WORLD BANK STAFF WORKING PAPERS
Number 792

On Shadow Pricing

Edward Tower
Garry Pursell

The World Bank
Washington, D.C., U.S.A.

Copyright © 1986
The International Bank for Reconstruction
and Development/THE WORLD BANK
1818 H Street, N.W.
Washington, D.C. 20433, U.S.A.

This is a working document published informally by the World Bank. To present the results of research with the least possible delay, the typescript has not been prepared in accordance with the procedures appropriate to formal printed texts, and the World Bank accepts no responsibility for errors. The publication is supplied at a token charge to defray part of the cost of manufacture and distribution.

The World Bank does not accept responsibility for the views expressed herein, which are those of the authors and should not be attributed to the World Bank or to its affiliated organizations. The findings, interpretations, and conclusions are the results of research supported by the Bank; they do not necessarily represent official policy of the Bank. The designations employed, the presentation of material, and any maps used in this document are solely for the convenience of the reader and do not imply the expression of any opinion whatsoever on the part of the World Bank or its affiliates concerning the legal status of any country, territory, city, area, or of its authorities, or concerning the delimitation of its boundaries, or national affiliation.

The most recent World Bank publications are described in the annual spring and fall lists; the continuing research program is described in the annual *Abstracts of Current Studies*. The latest edition of each is available free of charge from the Publications Sales Unit, Department T, The World Bank, 1818 H Street, N.W., Washington, D.C. 20433, U.S.A., or from the European Office of the Bank, 66 avenue d'Iéna, 75116 Paris, France.

Edward Tower is professor of economics at Duke University and a consultant to the World Bank; Garry Pursell is operational policy adviser in the Industrial Strategy and Policy Division of the Bank.

Library of Congress Cataloging-in-Publication Data

```
Tower, Edward.
   On shadow pricing.

   (World Bank staff working papers ; no. 792)
   Bibliography: p.
   1. Shadow prices.  2. Equilibrium (Economics)
I. Pursell, Garry.  II. Title.  III. Series.
HB143.T68  1986          338.5'2          85-29595
ISBN 0-8213-0695-2
```

ABSTRACT

The principal purpose of the monograph is to use general equilibrium methodology to explain the logical foundations of shadow prices and the techniques for deriving shadow price expressions. We first discuss the nature and meaning of shadow prices. Then we build a simple model in which each traded good is produced with intermediate inputs and a value added aggregate which are used in fixed proportions and with constant returns to scale, where the value added aggregate is a variable proportions function of a sector specific fixed factor and an intersectorally mobile factor of production which is common to all sectors. Using this model we first derive shadow prices for labor, traded goods, non-traded goods and foreign exchange assuming full employment and a flexible real exchange rate, with household welfare being held constant by adjustments in income taxes. The same basic approach is then extended to more complex models including models with alternative adjustment mechanisms. We also discuss how to shadow price factors, goods, policy parameters and autonomous parameters in terms of other goods whose shadow prices are known without having to solve a full-fledged general equilibrium model. This work explains the logical foundations of formulae in Squire and van der Tak (1975) and Ray (1984) and generalizes their approaches. The first three appendices comment from a general equilibrium perspective on some of the shadow price expressions proposed in three books on shadow pricing, while appendices D and E illustrate the kind of analysis that is needed if the models are so complex that they require matrix inversion.

ACKNOWLEDGEMENTS

This paper was written while Tower (who teaches at Duke University) was consulting with Garry Pursell at the World Bank's Industrial Development and Finance Department (which subsequently became the present Industrial Strategy and Policy Division of the Industry Department) in connection with the Incentives and Comparative Advantage (INCA) Unit research project (RPO672-44). The INCA Unit was established to support the many studies at the Bank and in developing countries, which involve the estimation of empirical incentive and cost-benefit (comparative advantage) indicators. The authors are grateful to the following people (both Bank staff members and others) for helpful comments: Clive Bell, Trent Bertrand, Phil Brock, Pat Conway, Shanta Devarajan, Kiyoun Han, Gordon Hughes, Glenn Jenkins, Kent Kimbrough, Elio Londero, Anandarup Ray, Neil Roger, Sudhir Shetty, and Lyn Squire. Thanks also go to Vivian Cherian for help provided at various stages and to Wanda Jedierowski, Pat Johnson, Stacy Miller and F.L. Smith for typing various versions.

TABLE OF CONTENTS

---

*Edward Tower is sole author of appendices A, B, and C.

Chapter I

INTRODUCTION

1. Overview

The purpose of this monograph is to illustrate by example what general equilibrium methodology has to tell us about calculating shadow prices for goods, factors of production, and foreign exchange and to provide a few new simple formulae which deal explicitly with the interindustry structure of production, variable world prices and non standard macroeconomic adjustment mechanisms. It has its genesis in Garry Pursell's (1978) paper which estimated shadow exchange rates for the Ivory Coast and Tower (1984). In essence, the monograph uses the approaches discussed in Tower's paper to make the derivations of the formulas in the Pursell paper more formal and to generalize them.[1]

Throughout the paper we keep the economic structure of the models considered fairly simple, assuming for the most part that each good is produced with intermediate inputs and a value added aggregate which are used in fixed

_____

[1] We developed most of these ideas before realizing that E. Sieper covered much of the same ground as we cover in our chapters I and II in an important unpublished paper in 1981. We share the same views as Sieper regarding the logic of shadow pricing. However, some of Sieper's shadow price expressions are reduced forms and others which are expressed in structural parameters require matrix inversion. Our expressions involve structural parameters and are derived under the assumption of specific demand and supply relationships which were used in order to generate simple expressions for shadow prices. Also, unlike Sieper, we explicitly incorporate the effective protection concept in our models.

The Jenkins-Kuo (forthcoming) paper also builds a model which is very close in spirit to ours, except that it employs the Armington assumption of imperfect substitution between domestically and foreign produced varieties of the same good.

proportions and with constant returns to scale. Then we permit the value added aggregate to be a constant returns to scale, variable proportions function of a fixed factor which is specific to the sector which employs it and a factor which is mobile between sectors. Thus we can think of the model as describing a short-run equilibrium where the capital stock is the fixed factor and labor is the mobile factor: this is the terminology we will use throughout the paper.

There is, however, an alternative interpretation of the model which makes it a reasonable description of an economy in long run equilibrium. We can think of capital services as being like any other intermediate input. The simplest assumption we could make is that capital is available on the world capital market at a fixed real interest rate or that the supply of domestic savings is perfectly elastic, and that there is an international market in used machinery so that a machine can be easily converted into foreign exchange. Then we could assume that the fixed factor in each sector is sector specific managerial or technical skill with less skilled or more-generally skilled labor being the intersectorally mobile factor of production in limited aggregate supply. Alternatively, we may interpret the fixed factor as being a limited quantity of venture capital in each sector created either by a desire for portfolio diversification or else a moral hazard problem which means that managers must provide their own risk capital. Thus, we believe that our model is quite a useful one in that it can be interpreted to fit a wide range of circumstances.

While we do work entirely with one mobile primary factor the only reason we do this is to obtain tractable formulae, but if one is willing to settle for more complex formulae which involve matrix inversion, one can introduce an unlimited number of mobile factors.

The result which emerges from all but one of our formulae is that deviations of our shadow prices from market prices turn out to be weighted averages of distortions in production and consumption with the weights based on supply and compensated demand elasticities and other parameters describing the base equilibrium. The exception is the shadow price of foreign exchange in utility numeraire which also requires knowledge of marginal propensities to spend. Moreover, in our simplest models, with no domestic distortions and fixed world prices, these distortions are simply effective tariffs and nominal tariffs. Also, reassuringly, the shadow prices of traded goods which have fixed world prices attached simply turn out to be those fixed world prices.

Much of the paper is quite mathematical. This is inevitable because we wish to emphasize the logical foundations of the shadow prices we derive, as well as the techniques used to derive them, as opposed to writing a cook book for the project evaluator. Still, the paper should have use as a cookbook, for certain formulae are developed which are unavailable elsewhere and are quite simple and useful. For a discussion of the mathematical tools used, which would also serve as an introduction to the ideas developed here, the reader is referred to chapters II and V of Tower (1984).

A reader's guide is appropriate. In Chapters I and II we use a simple model, which lends itself to the use of geometric reasoning, to lay out the main ideas of the paper, namely how to think about shadow prices and how to derive them in some simple cases. Chapter III discusses the how to shadow price goods, factors, policy parameters and autonomous non-policy parameters in terms of the shadow prices of other goods, which are assumed to be known. It also discusses the logic of various different types of conversion factors and shows how to use them in shadow pricing one item in terms of other items. Chapter IV builds a set of tools for the formal derivation of shadow prices which we then apply in chapters IV and V and VI to derive shadow prices under various assumptions. The first three appendices consist of sets of comments on pieces dealing with problems of shadow pricing which cost some effort to understand. Finally, Appendices D and E illustrate the kind of analysis that can be done if one is willing to use models that are sufficiently complex to require matrix inversion.

Many readers will wish to read through chapter IV and skip lightly over the rest of the monograph, since chapters V and VI are similar in construction to IV, except that the assumptions used and formulae derived there are different. The first three of the appendices will interest only those readers who are concerned with the literature considered there, and the last two appendices indicate the sort of methodology that one can use with more complex models rather than coming up with particular formulae that one would be likely to want to apply.

We now provide a non-technical summary of the issues involved in shadow pricing and the results of the monograph. Those readers who are already familiar with the basic ideas of shadow pricing may wish to skim the rest of this chapter, and pick up the model in chapter II where it is laid out more tersely.

2. A Non-technical Introduction to the Issues Involved in Shadow Pricing and the Results of The Monograph

a. The Model

In order to understand the meaning of the shadow prices we are about to derive it is convenient to work initially with the very simple model economy which is illustrated schematically in figure 1. It consists of households

Figure 1

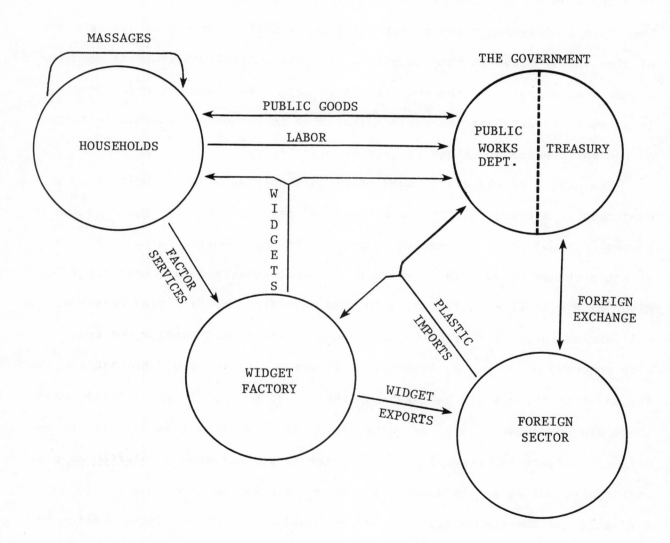

which supply a fixed quantity of labor for the production of traded goods (widgets), non-traded labor services (massages), and public goods supplied by the government. As we have noted previously, labor is the sole intersectorally mobile factor of production.

To produce widgets, labor and an imported intermediate input (plastic)are combined with a fixed quantity of sector specific capital. This means that there are diminishing returns to the application of labor and an upward sloping supply curve in this industry. In this initial and simplest model we assume that widgets are the country's sole export and that our model country is so small relative to the world market that it has no perceptible influence on the world price of either widgets or plastic.

The export of widgets is subject to an export subsidy at the rate τ, expressed as a fraction of the world price, p^*. More precisely, p^* is the border (f.o.b.) price of widgets (expressed in the domestic currency at the market exchange rate). The ex-factory price of widgets sold domestically is given by $p = p^*(1 + \tau)$. While in this case the domestic price of widgets will exceed the border price by the amount of the export subsidy, we could also conceive of τ as an export tax, in which case τ would be negative and the domestic price would be less than the export price. In the initial model there are no domestic sales or value added taxes, so that p is also the price paid for widgets by households. In chapter II we introduce a value-added tax on widgets, but as we shall see the same principles continue to apply to the derivation of the shadow prices. The assumption that the ex-factory price of widgets is also the consumer price means that there are no wholesale or retail margins (which is also implied by our assumption that "massages" is the only non-traded activity). Furthermore, the production of widgets is assumed to require no non-traded intermediate inputs, an assumption which (as demonstrated in appendices D and E) does not alter any essential principles, but does simplify the shadow price expressions.

Widget production requires an intermediate input ("plastic") which is used in fixed technical proportions and which is imported at a given world (c.i.f.) price. The assumption of fixed technical raw material input-output coefficients is not needed when relative prices of all primary and intermediate factors are fixed, but dropping it would complicate things in models where these relative prices vary. Our rationale for keeping it is the standard one that substitution between individual material inputs and between material inputs and components of value added is probably low or in any event sufficiently low and sufficiently difficult to estimate as to be a minor source of error relative to others, in empirical applications. In this initial model plastic is the economy's sole import, so that the balance of trade in any given period is simply the difference between the border value of widget exports and plastic imports. In later versions of the model (e.g., chapter II), we relax this assumption by allowing for domestic production of both intermediate inputs such as plastics and importable consumer goods other than widgets, as well as for the import of consumer goods which are not produced domestically, and we show that these extensions do not change any of our essential conclusions about shadow prices and leave us with very similar expressions for them.

In the production of non-traded services, we initially assume that labor is the sole input (hence "massages"). This means that the price of these services is simply the wage rate, given our assumption of a competitive labor market. Later, in chapter III, we allow for intermediate material inputs used in the production of non-traded goods and services, and finally for the existence of sector specific capital, which implies diminishing returns and an upward sloping supply curve in the production of non-tradeds. Since this in turn means that changes in the demand for non-tradeds are accompanied by changes in their prices we show that the shadow price formulas become correspondingly more complex.

In our simple model, the government collects taxes which it uses to pay for the production of various public services, and it holds the country's foreign exchange reserves. The taxes are income taxes on households plus net receipts from trade taxes and subsidies, i.e., the difference between receipts from the import duties on plastic minus the export subsidies on widgets. Obviously, depending on the relative importance of import tariffs and export subsidies, trade taxes could represent a net outlay rather than net income for the government. The government itself is envisaged as an abstract entity employing labor and other factors to produce an exogenously fixed supply of various public goods such as defense, health and education services, etc. Since there is no saving in our model, these services are financed through taxes rather than borrowing. However, the results in no way depend on the existence of a minimal Adam Smith style government. There is no reason that the government should not also own part or even all of the capital in the sectors producing traded goods, (and in the non-traded sectors once sector-specific capital is introduced) provided only that the market structures remain competitive and production and pricing decisions continue to be made in accordance with profit maximising principles.[1] Compared with our simple model, the only difference would be that government income would include a profit component while the taxable income of households would be lower to the

---

[1]Actually imperfect competition does not destroy the applicability of the analysis because a monopolist/monopolist can be thought of as a perfect competitor who attaches implicit taxes to his output and use of inputs with upward sloping supplies. For more on this see Tower (1984, sec. V.8.a).

same extent. Operating losses requiring subsidies or operating surpluses by government enterprises could also be handled by treating them as negative or positive sales taxes, although only value added taxes, not those particular taxes, are dealt with in our paper.

As regards households, as noted previously, we assume that the total quantity of labor supplied is fixed over the relevant range of variation of prices, real wages and income taxes. This assumption simplifies the analysis by doing away with the need to treat leisure as a consumption good, the demand for which would depend on these variables.[1] In particular, changes in income taxes are assumed to have no effect on the labor supply. Real income or welfare is assumed not to depend on the distribution of income between households. Also, households are assumed to be utility maximisers, so that in equilibrium the marginal utilities of the goods they consume will be proportional to their prices. Thus, a change in the standard of living (or national welfare), dy, is defined as the change in the consumption of goods by households dC_i multiplied by their consumer prices p_i^c. That is $dy = \Sigma p_i^c \cdot dC_i$. In effect we treat all households together as though they are one single household. While utility maximisation is necessary for legitimate use of our welfare criterion and hence for the formulae we develop, the simple aggregation of households is not essential, although information requirements and the complexity of shadow price expressions would increase if welfare weights depending on the distribution of real incomes between households were

---

[1]Alternatively one may think of "massages" as leisure and pretend that widgets are the only marketed goods which are consumed.

introduced.[1] The dC_i are assumed to include "private" goods only (which as noted above could be produced by government owned corporations) as distinct from the "public' goods and services such as defense, law and order, etc. which are supplied free of charge by the government. While the latter affect the <u>absolute</u> level of the standard of living, since the quantity supplied is constant, they have no effect on <u>changes</u> in the standard of living.

In order to further simplify our model, we assume that there is no private saving - all disposable household income after the payment of income taxes is fully spent on traded goods (widgets) or non-traded labor services (massages). Since there is no change in government expenditure on public goods, any change in net government income must be accompanied by an equal increase or decrease in the foreign exchange reserves held by the government (valuing the change in foreign exchange holdings in "border pesos").[2]

We now imagine that the possibility of undertaking a new project arises. The project could be either undertaken directly by the government, or could be undertaken privately provided government permission (and perhaps a subsidy) is given. To simplify, we can assume that the project will export a product not consumed domestically (say a mineral), so that in order to know whether it is economically worthwhile undertaking, the government will need to compare the foreign exchange shadow value of the inputs which will be needed

─────────────────

[1]Alternatively, we can recognize that income distribution is a variable of concern to the policymaker, but that he or she has already adjusted the income tax, so that at the margin changes in the income distribution do not matter. In other words, the policymaker uses the income tax to optimize the income distribution and project evaluation to maximize efficiency, which as Harberger (1978a; 1978b) argues is a sensible solution of this assignment problem.

[2]This result follows from the fact that since the private sector spends all of its disposable income its budget is always in balance. Therefore, the government's budget deficit must be equal to the foreign sector's budget surplus, i.e., the rate at which the government loses reserves.

to produce it, with the foreign exchange which would be earned by the exports. This means that the government will need to know the shadow prices of labor, traded products (widgets and plastics), and non-traded services and products (massages) which the project may require. In the following sections we first discuss the shadow price of labor in some detail, as a way of illustrating how our model works. We then discuss in turn the shadow pricing of traded products and non-traded services and products. Next, we discuss the shadow price of foreign exchange itself in terms of the standard of living or "utility numeraire." Finally we summarize how the shadow prices would be used to evaluate the project, and provide a succinct summary of some principal conclusions of later chapters.

b. The Shadow Price of Labor

A simple story that illustrates the meaning of the shadow price of labor is the following. Consider an economy with a fixed set of tariffs, export taxes and subsidies. The government is contemplating a project which requires one man-day of labor to produce one dollar's worth of foreign exchange, and wants to know if it should undertake the project. To answer this question we need to know how many dollars a man-day of labor is worth. To figure that out we need to know the rate at which the government is able to convert man-days into dollars by alternative means.

The standard story implicit in most analyses but explicit in few is the following. The government stands ready to hire labor at the going market wage. It can induce the private sector to release labor by revaluing the currency, and holding the money wage constant, which will create some unemployed labor (which now seeks employment in the public sector) while using up foreign exchange and raising or lowering the standard of living. Then by adjusting the income tax, the government can put the standard of living back to where it was before. Once this has worked itself out, the ratio of the change in foreign exchange used to the labor released by the private sector is noted and defined as the shadow price of labor, for it is the amount of foreign exchange that the government must pay to the private sector to compensate it for each unit of labor released. If and only if our project converts labor into foreign exchange on better terms than this is it a good thing. Moreover, by definition this will be the case if and only if the foreign exchange earned exceeds the cost of the labor used when valued at its shadow price.

This can be spelled out in more detail using our simple widget-massage model. As the exchange rate is revalued, the widget processing margin is squeezed and production is cut back, releasing labor. At the same time, since the domestic consumer price of widgets falls, household demand is diverted from massages to widgets, thus releasing additional labor from the massage sector. What is the impact of this on household real income (welfare)? On the one hand, since the price of widgets has declined while the price of massages has not changed, real income will have increased. On the other hand, the reduced return to the specific factor (measured in units of domestic currency) will have lowered household nominal income even if the government hires the surplus labor in the project at the same wage.[1] In this simple model, since there is only one traded product which is being exported, there

---

[1]Since we are testing whether or not the project ought to be undertaken, the labor is obviously not yet employed in the project. Indeed, unless the project is actually undertaken, none of the above actually happens. We are rather estimating what would happen if the project were to go ahead.

must be a decrease in real income.[1] The government now cuts income taxes so as to restore household real income to its previous level, which will increase spending on widgets and massages. This will result in some increase in massage production and some re-employment of labor there, while in the widget sector there will be a further reduction in exports but no change in production or employment. In the final equilibrium the amount of labor released from widget production will depend on the elasticity of supply of widgets, and the amount of labor released from massage production will depend on how closely widgets substitute for massages in household consumption, i.e., on the income-compensated cross elasticity of demand between widgets and massages. What is the effect of all this on foreign exchange reserves? First, the reduction in widget production will lead to a decline in net foreign exchange earnings equal to the difference between the export value of the reduced production of widgets, minus the c.i.f. value of the reduction in plastic imports which are used to produce the widgets. Secondly, the switch of household consumption demand from massages to widgets will lead to a decline in foreign exchange reserves equal to the export value of the extra widgets which are now consumed domestically. Again, the importance of these two effects will depend respectively on the supply elasticity of widgets and the compensated cross elasticity of demand between widgets and massages. As pointed out previously, the ratio of the net decline in foreign exchange reserves to the amount of labor released is defined as the shadow price of labor, since it shows how much extra foreign exchange is required to maintain the standard of living while withdrawing a unit of labor from producing traded and non-traded goods for use in the project.

---

[1]If there is more than one traded product, some of which are being imported and some exported, real income may increase or decrease.

In the adjustment process we have just described, the government operates on the exchange rate and the income tax, while the nominal wage remains unchanged. We get the same results if the exchange rate is fixed and the nominal wage is allowed to vary with constancy of the living standard again maintained by varying the income tax. In this scenario, the government hires the labor it requires for the project, which has the effect of forcing up the nominal wage, thus leading to a reduction in widget production (which faces unchanged widget and plastic prices) and a switch of consumption from massages (whose price has increased) to widgets. The inital net effect is again to decrease real household income, so the government decreases income taxes in order to restore the initial level of household real income. In the final equilibrium the amount of labor released and the compensating rundown of foreign exchange reserves will depend as before on the elasticity of the supply of widgets and the compensated cross elasticity of demand between massages and widgets.

We again get the same result if we assume that, following the withdrawal of labor, wage flexibility and the effect of price changes on the real value of money balances held by households (the real balance effect) are such that full employment of the remaining labor and balance of payments equilibrium are automatically maintained at a given exchange rate. In this case, in order to keep real household income unchanged, the government again releases foreign exchange, which we can conceive as being done indirectly by reducing income taxes, thereby inducing increased household expenditure and decreased exports of widgets.

c. The Shadow Price of Labor Continued:

A Simple Geometric Illustration

The verbal description for deriving the shadow price of labor is illustrated for the simplest widget massage model in Figure 2. The two related diagrams show the demand and supply conditions for widgets, using the following definitions:

p = domestic currency price of widgets (in pesos)

p^* = foreign currency price of widgets (in dollars or border pesos)

v = unit value added in widgets measured in domestic currency (in pesos)

v^* = unit value added in widgets measured in foreign currency (in dollars or border pesos)

p^* PLASTIC = foreign currency price of enough plastic to produce one widget

α = the proportion by which the domestic currency is appreciated

o = before appreciation

1 = after appreciation

plastic =the intermediate input

η = compensated elasticity of demand

e = elasticity of supply

16

Figure 2

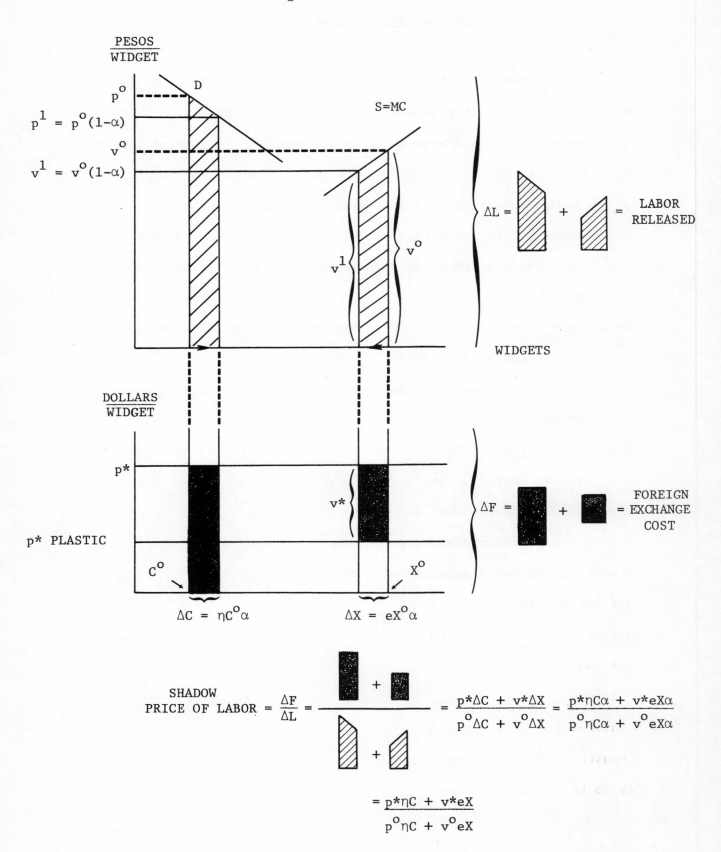

The initial equilibrium is shown by the intersection of the dotted lines and the supply and demand curves in the upper part of the diagram where p^o is the initial domestic peso price of a widget, and v^o is the initial domestic peso value-added per widget. Since labor is the sole variable primary factor, and plastic is used in fixed proportions with widgets, the quantity supplied is determined by the height of the available processing margin, v^o, and the marginal labor cost per widget (the value-added supply curve S). Note that D is the income compensated demand curve for widgets, i.e., it represents household demand for widgets given by varying prices while holding household real income constant by income tax adjustments.

In order to release labor, we now suppose as before that the government appreciates the peso by the proportion α, while simultaneously adjusting the income tax so as to keep real household income unchanged. As a result, the widget price declines, resulting in a switch of demand from massage to widget consumption. The resulting increase in widget consumption, ΔC, depends on the compensated cross elasticity of demand between widgets and massages, η, and the proportionate revaluation α, i.e., specifically $\Delta C = \eta C^o \alpha$. Looking at the bottom part of the diagram, we can see that an amount of foreign exchange equal to the shaded area on the left is used up, since $p^* \Delta C$ worth of widgets are no longer exported. Note that this foreign exchange loss can be measured directly in foreign currency, or alternatively it could be measured in "border pesos," as long as the latter is defined in terms of the same exchange rate (most conveniently, as in this paper, in terms of the initial exchange rate). Looking at the top part of the diagram, the cross-hatched area under the compensated demand curve is the value of the extra household utility generated by increased consumption of widgets and for utility to be constant, it must be matched by an equal reduction in expenditure on massages. Since massages are provided entirely by labor services, this area, which for (small α) is approximately equal to $p^o \Delta C$, can be used to represent the amount of labor released as a result of the expenditure switch, where a unit of labor is defined as that amount whose wage is one peso.[1]

Turning now to the supply reaction, the peso appreciation squeezes the value-added margin available for transforming the imported plastic into widgets by the same proportion α, from v^o to v^1. As a result production is cut back by ΔX which depends on initial widget supply X^o, the elasticity of supply of widgets with respect to the price of value added (or the wage rate) e, and the proportionate appreciation α. The consequent foreign exchange loss is shown as the shaded area, and is equal to the foreign currency (or border peso) unit value added, v*, multiplied by ΔX. Corresponding to this, an amount of labor represented by the cross hatched area under S is released, which is approximately equal to $v^o \Delta X$, or the change in value added expressed in domestic pesos.

Putting the demand and supply reactions together as shown in Figure 2 gives an expression which shows the total amount of foreign exchange released from reserves divided by the domestic peso value of the labor released from producing massages and widgets. Since the denominator represents labor units, dividing the numerator by the denominator gives the foreign exchange shadow price of labor.

So far we have not explicitly referred to the effects of the export subsidy on widgets and the import duty on plastic. From now on, v* and p*

---

[1] For example, if the area is equivalent to 1000 pesos, and the hourly wage is 10 pesos, the area would be equivalent to the release of 100 hours of labor. More generally, in the rest of the paper we simply normalize the wage rate at unity, so that a unit of labor is defined as that amount which earns 1 peso in the initial equilibrium.

will be measured in border pesos. First we have $p^o = p^* (1+\tau)$, i.e., the domestic widget price is equal to its border peso price plus the export subsidy at the rate of τ . Secondly:

$$v^o = v^* (1 + ERP)$$

i.e., unit value added in domestic pesos is equal to unit value added in border pesos multiplied by one plus the effective rate of protection, where ERP expresses the combined effect of the export subsidy and the import duty on plastic.

The expressions for p^o and v^o can now be substituted in the denominator of the shadow price expression to give for the shadow price of labor:

$$SPL = \frac{\eta p^*C + ev^*X}{(1+\tau)\eta p^*C + (1+ERP)ev^*X} \qquad (1)$$

where we have dropped the "o" superscripts on C and X. Thus the nominal protection (τ) and the effective protection for widgets (ERP) enter directly into the expression for the shadow price of labor.

Assume that $\tau = .2$ and ERP = .4. Then take the extreme case where ηp^*C is zero or very small relative to ev^*X (for example, widgets are not consumed locally at all, or are very poor substitutes for massages). Then

$$SPL = 1/(1+ERP) = 1/(1+.4) = .71 \qquad (2)$$

That is, one domestic peso's worth of labor has a shadow price of .71 border pesos. Now take the opposite case where ev^*X is zero or very small relative to ηp^*C. Then

$$SPL = 1/(1+\tau) = 1/(1+.2) = .83. \tag{3}$$

If we take intermediate cases, in which labor is withdrawn from both widgets and massages, we will need to plug in values for the other terms in the expression, but if the nominal and effective protection are as above, the shadow price will fall between these two limiting cases. For example, using $\tau = .2$ and ERP = .4 again, and arbitrary values for the other variables as indicated, we get:

$$SPL = \frac{[(.5)(10)(20)] + [(1)(5)(30)]}{(1.2)[(.5)(10)(20)] + (1.4)[(1)(5)(30)]} = .76 \tag{4}$$

In this example the greater is the weight of the adjustment via widget production relative to that by widget consumption, the lower is the shadow price (conversion factor) for labor. The 40% effective protection of widget production being greater than its 20% nominal protection means that the withdrawal of a given amount of labor from widget production involves a relatively smaller net foreign exchange loss than does withdrawal of the same amount of labor from massage production with the same amount of consumption expenditure shifted into widgets. Hence, if widgets are close substitutes for massages in household consumption, so that there is a substantial switch of consumption from massages to widgets, the foreign exchange loss is larger.

Many discussions describe the shadow price of labor as a weighted average of the marginal products of labor valued at shadow prices. See, for example, Little and Mirrlees (1974, pp. 169-176), Mashayekhi (1980, pp. 51-54) and Powers (1981, pp. 34-35). This would seem to contradict the approach we use here, but in fact it doesn't. As we show in section III.2, the shadow wage rate will be equal to the sum of the increases in net outputs that would result from the government's release of one unit of labor, with each evaluated at its shadow price, assuming that the government holds the prices of all goods fixed by absorbing any excess supplies and satisfying any excess demands that are thereby created, and that it uses factor specific adjustments in income taxes and subsidies to keep disposable factor incomes unchanged. To see that this proposition holds true in our simple model, note that at constant widget, plastic and massage prices any excess supplies of labor released by the government will flow into massages, because the derived demand for labor services in widgets is downward sloping due to the sector-specific capital employed in widgets, whereas with the massage price held constant by government policy, the derived demand for labor in massages is perfectly elastic at the initial wage. This means that the shadow price of labor is the same as the shadow price of massages, which we know to be true since in essence they are the same thing.

As we show in section IV.2, there are yet two additional ways to view the shadow price of labor which are consistent with our modeling here. In that section, we define reference prices of factors and non-traded goods as their market prices to suppliers, and reference prices of traded goods as their marginal rates of transformation into foreign exchange on world markets. Then we note that the shadow price of a good or a factor is its reference price plus the weighted sum of changes in factor service flows and the changes in consumption induced by government release of a unit of the good or factor service in question, assuming the government holds real income constant by varying its holdings of foreign exchange. For factor service flows the weights are the differences between unit value added at reference and market price, and for consumption expenditure the weights are the differences between prices to consumers and reference prices.

Also, in section IV.2, yet another expression for the shadow price of labor views it as the sum of the induced changes in net outputs weighted by reference prices plus the sum of changed consumption weighted by the differences between consumer prices and reference prices, where again these induced changes follow from release of a unit of the factor services by the government, and the government is presumed to hold real income constant by varying income taxes.

d.   Shadow Pricing Traded Goods

We now suppose that the project also requires widgets and plastics as inputs. If the project simply buys the widgets, foreign exchange reserves will decline by the export value of the widgets, while there will be no change in household real income since there is no change in household money income and no change in the price of widgets or in the price of massages. Hence the shadow price of a widget is simply its border price (in this example f.o.b.). It is also easy to see that the decline in foreign exchange reserves is equal to the decline in net government income, since there is no change in government revenue while government expenditure has increased by the domestic price of a widget minus the per-widget export subsidy. Similarly, if the government buys plastic (say from local importers) foreign exchange reserves decline by the c.i.f. value of the increased plastic imports, while again there is no change in household real income. The net reduction in government income is equal to the domestic price of a unit of plastic minus the extra import duty collected, i.e., it is the same as the foreign exchange shadow price or border price of the plastic.

In the simple widget-massage model, it is assumed that the country is a price taker in the world markets for widgets and plastics, so that the decline in foreign exchange reserves when they are used by a project is simply the quantity used multiplied by the border price. However, if the country is a sufficiently large exporter or importer of a particular product, it may sometimes happen that changes in its imports or exports will lead to changes in the world price. In the case of importables, this means that foreign exchange reserves will decline by more than the border price multiplied by the increase in imports, and in the case of exportables it means that foreign exchange reserves will rise by less than the increase in exports multiplied by the border price. Hence it might appear that the foreign exchange shadow price of an importable is equal to its marginal foreign exchange cost to the economy, which will exceed its border price, while the shadow price of an exportable might appear to be equal to its marginal foreign exchange revenue to the economy, which will be less than its border price. However, this is not correct since the variability of border prices means that prices of these goods to households will also vary. As discussed in Chapter IV, this complicates the expressions for estimating the shadow prices of these traded goods as well as the shadow prices of labor and non-traded goods.

e. Shadow Pricing Non-Traded Goods and Services

In our simplest widget-massage model, since a unit of the non-traded service "massages" is identical with a unit of labor, it is evident that the shadow price of massages must be the same as the shadow price of labor which we have already discussed at some length. The shadow pricing of a non-traded good or service becomes more complex, however, when we go beyond this very simple model. Suppose that, like widgets, massages are produced with a sector-specific factor (say capital) and variable labor, so that the massage supply curve is upward sloping. Suppose also that the project will need to buy a certain quantity of massages. Since all labor is already fully employed the extra massages must come from increased production of massages using labor diverted from widget production, plus reduced household consumption of massages. If wages are flexible and the exchange rate is not varied, this would be brought about by the increased demand for massages leading to an increase in money wages and an increase in the market price of massages. Suppose that the initial net effect would be to increase real household income, and that the government increases income taxes so as to leave real income unchanged. In the new equilibrium the massages required by the project would come in part from increased production and in part from reduced consumption by households resulting from the increase in the price of massages relative to the widget price, which is fixed at its border price plus the export subsidy, and is therefore unchanged. The corresponding run-down of foreign exchange reserves consists, firstly, of the net foreign exchange cost of reduced widget production which results from increased money wages, combined with an unchanged domestic-peso processing margin in widget production. This cutback of widget production (and exports) releases the labor required for the increased production of massages, of which the marginal foreign exchange cost is simply the amount of labor transferred times its foreign exchange opportunity cost in producing widgets. The second component of the run-down in foreign exchange reserves results from the switch of household consumption from massages to widgets. Its relative importance will depend (as in our discussion of the shadow price of labor) on the compensated cross elasticity of demand between massages and widgets (η), supply elasticities of the two goods and on the nominal export subsidy rate on widgets (τ).

The story told above assumes that the exchange rate is not varied so that labor market balance and unchanged living standards result from flexible wages combined with income tax adjustments. At the other extreme the government might appreciate the peso in such a way as to maintain supply and demand balance in the labor market without any change in money wages, while once again adjusting the income tax to maintain the real standard of living. Since in this story relative prices change in the same way as previously (in both cases we have a real currency appreciation) it is not surprising that the foreign exchange run-down associated with the purchase of the non-traded services for the project is identical, i.e., we get an identical expression for the shadow price of massages.

f. Shadow Pricing Foreign Exchange in Utility Numeraire

Now let's ask about a different kind of project. This one involves spending a dollar of foreign exchange to create one peso's worth of increased standard of living, i.e. producer's and consumer's surplus, real income, or utility measured as $\sum_i p_i dC_i$ where p_i is the price of the ith good to consumers and C_i is consumption of it. This is a good thing only if this project does a better job than the standard macropolicy of converting foreign exchange to utility. How do we define that standard? We appreciate the currency, cut taxes by enough to keep the economy at full employment, note the ratio of the change in utility generated to the foreign exchange used and call it the shadow price of foreign exchange in utility numeraire, or, for short, the shadow price of foreign exchange. If this is less than the corresponding ratio for the project, we undertake the project. The reciprocal of this shadow price is the foreign exchange required to increase utility by one unit and is defined as the conversion factor for real income.

Once again it is useful to spell this out by going back to our simple widget-massage model. Let us suppose that the government wishes to increase real household income by one peso. As long as there are no price changes, it can do this by reducing income taxes by one peso. Suppose that this is the case because households would spend the extra peso entirely on traded goods. In our simple model, this means that the peso would be spent on widgets, and would lead to a reduction of widget exports (expressed in border pesos) of $1/(1+\tau)$. This would then be the conversion factor for real income (c_y), since it shows the amount of foreign exchange required to increase real income by one peso. Its reciprocal, $1 + \tau$, is the shadow price of foreign exchange (SPFX) since it shows the change in real household income which would result from the release of one border peso from foreign exchange reserves.

More generally, if all incremental household disposable income were spent on traded goods, the conversion factor for real income would be

$$c_y = \Sigma \frac{m_i}{1 + \tau_i} \quad , \tag{5}$$

where the m_i are the marginal propensities to spend on traded goods, and $\Sigma m_i = 1$. Once again, SPFX would equal the reciprocal of this expression.

In practice, however, a good part of incremental disposable household income will be spent on non-traded goods and services, as well as on traded goods. In this case (as we show in Chapter II), in order to calculate the amount of foreign exchange used, we can multiply the marginal propensity to spend on each non-traded good by its foreign exchange shadow price. In the simple widget-massage model, this would give

$$c_y = \frac{m_w}{1 + \tau} + m_\ell \cdot SPL \qquad (6)$$

where m_w and m_ℓ are the marginal propensities to spend on widgets and labor services, $m_w + m_\ell = 1$ and SPL is the shadow price or conversion factor for labor (identical in this case to the shadow price of massages) as discussed previously.

Going back to our discussion of the shadow price of labor and non-traded goods, it is obvious that as soon as we allow for incremental expenditure on non-traded goods, the expression for c_y and its reciprocal SPFX will become much more complex, simply because the expressions for the shadow prices of non-traded goods are more complex than those for traded goods. This is because additional expenditure on non-tradeds has to be met by increased production. In the widget-massage model, this means that labor has to be withdrawn from widget production, which is brought about by an appreciation in the exchange rate, so that the foreign exchange used depends in part on the production adjustment in the widget industry and so on the supply elasticity in the widget industry and its effective protection. Because of the reduction in the relative price of widgets, additional foreign exchange is also used up by substitution of widgets for massages in household expenditure.

This subject is discussed in more detail in later chapters but it is worth making a few general points in advance.

First, given that in any real economy the marginal propensity to spend on non-tradeds will not be zero, the eventual increase in foreign exchange spent to increase real income by one peso will be higher than the sum of the shadow prices (conversion factors) for traded goods weighted by their m_i since there will be a substitution of tradeds for non-traded goods in household expenditure due to the higher prices of non-traded goods resulting from increased demand combined with upward sloping supply and also due to the fact that labor will be released from the traded sectors.

Secondly, while expressions for c_y or SPFX involving only traded goods can be derived, the elasticities in these expressions must be understood as general equilibrium elasticities, i.e., they express the changes in the demand and supply of traded goods after all the general equilibrium effects have worked themselves out.

Thirdly, given that c_y and SPFX depend on marginal propensities to spend, it is obvious that they will vary according to which group of consumers benefit from the increase in real income (tax cut) as soon as we no longer treat all households together as though they are a single household.

Finally, c_y and SPFX will also be different if adjustment mechanisms other than real currency appreciation are used to release resources from the traded sectors.

g. Putting It All Together

The typical project will involve using labor, foreign exchange, and some goods to produce other goods, a change in utility, and a change in foreign exchange. Weighting the net increases in supplies of the various goods by their shadow prices, subtracting the quantity of labor used weighted by its shadow price and then adding the change in utility multiplied by the real income conversion factor gives the gross benefits, measured in foreign exchange, of the project. Subtracting the foreign exchange used up gives the net benefit measured in foreign exchange. To calculate the net benefit of the project in real income (or utility) numeraire, the net benefit measured in foreign exchange is multiplied by the shadow price of foreign exchange. The project is desirable if and only if the net benefit calculated with either numeraire is positive.

h. Summary of the Monograph's Major Results

In the paper, we show what kinds of assumptions are needed to make the calculations of such shadow prices tractable and we calculate various shadow price formulae. Some specific results are the following.

As we know from Blitzer, Dasgupta and Stiglitz (1981) and Bell and Devarajan (1983) shadow prices depend on the adjustment mechanisms assumed. If the adjustment mechanism is a tariff change rather than an exchange-rate change and/or an excise tax change rather than an income tax change, the shadow prices are different. We present examples where the adjustment mechanism is an income tax change combined with a change in certain tariffs and/or effective rates of protection.

It is easiest to calculate shadow prices using the specific factor model with one mobile factor of production and assuming that certain compensated cross price demand elasticities are zero. We present several different sets of assumptions that work to make life easy for us. The precise assumptions in each chapter's model are laid out in their introductions, so we will not repeat them here.

When world prices are fixed and there are no nontradeable goods except for labor services, our shadow price formulae involve effective rates of protection (ERPs) and nominal tariffs.

When world prices are variable or there are non-traded goods we use concepts that are closely related to ERPs and nominal tariffs, but differ slightly. Our nominal tariffs are replaced by differences between consumer prices and reference prices. For traded goods reference prices are marginal rates of transformation into foreign exchange. This then is a marginal revenue concept for exports and marginal expenditure concept for imports, rather than price, and for non-traded goods, these reference prices are prices received by producers. Finally, we replace the traditional ERP by a new concept that is calculated as the old concept would be except that the reference prices in the new concept replace world prices in the old. Thus the ith ERP in the new concept shows the proportion by which value added at prices paid and received by a producer of the ith good exceeds the value added measured at reference prices.

Finally, we develop some simple formulae which enable us to derive shadow prices of some items in terms of other items, be they goods, factors or parameters. This may obviate the need to solve a full-fledged general equilibrium system, when it is desired to calculate a few more shadow prices in a system where a number of shadow prices are already known.

Chapter II

A GEOMETRIC APPROACH TO SHADOW PRICING LABOR IN TERMS
OF FOREIGN EXCHANGE AND DERIVING THE SHADOW PRICE
OF FOREIGN EXCHANGE IN UTILITY NUMERAIRE

1. Introduction

In this chapter we first use the simple model which was introduced in
chapter I. Then we generalize the model to consider many traded goods. In
the first model the economy produces only two goods: non-traded labor
services (massages) and a traded manufactured good, widgets. Widgets are
produced using a value added aggregate and a bundle of imported intermediate
inputs in fixed proportions, where the value added aggregate is produced by
combining sector specific capital with labor, while massages are produced
using labor alone. Alternatively, we may rationalize the sector specific
factor as sector specific managerial skill or venture capital and treat the
capital stock as an intermediate input. Both widgets and massages are
consumed at home, so that labor in our model represents both the sole
intersectorally mobile factor of production and the sole non-traded good.
Finally, some widgets must be exported to pay for the imported intermediate
goods used in their production.

Using this model we show how to shadow price labor, first assuming that
exchange-rate or relative price adjustment is the mechanism by which foreign
exchange is allocated, then assuming that wages are inflexible and that taxes
or subsidies on trade or production are the mechanisms used. Then we discuss
how to use these results to obtain the shadow price of foreign exchange in

utility numeraire.

In the process, we show how to use effective rates of protection in calculating these shadow prices[1], provide a proof of a proposition of Scott (1974) and resolve the meaning of a formula designed by Balassa (1974) to describe the shadow price of foreign exchange and the conversion factor for primary factors of production.

2. On Targets, Instruments and Tradeoffs: The Logical Structure of The Model

It is important for understanding the meaning of the shadow prices we are about to derive to understand the model of economic policy which underlies their derivation. Throughout the paper we will pretend that all private final demand is consumption and assume away private international capital flows. Conceptually, it is possible to pretend that we have a Keynesian model with a rigid money wage and two instruments of economic policy: an exchange rate that the government can influence by official intervention, and income tax rates which the government can also vary. The government has three potential targets. The first is real income, y, defined by $dy = \sum p_i dC_i$ where C_i is consumption of the ith good, p_i is its price to consumers and the i in this instance runs over all goods including labor services, so dy is the change in aggregate consumption at consumer prices. The other two potential targets are the balance of payments, -F, (where -F is official savings of foreign exchange) and full employment. The two instruments can be set to achieve target values for any two of the three targets. We define the shadow price of

---

[1] In this regard, the paper extends Bertrand (1974) and Pursell (1978).

foreign exchange in utility numeraire (which we will calculate shortly) as the amount of increased y that the government can get for each unit of F, foreign exchange sacrificed, while keeping the economy at full employment, through the appropriate behind the scenes use of the two instruments. Similarly, the shadow price of labor shows how much the payments balance would have to deteriorate every time one worker leaves employment in the private sector if both the remaining workers are to remain fully employed and real income is to be held constant by appropriate changes in the levels of these two instruments. Such a shadow price is sometimes referred to as a shadow price in foreign exchange numeraire or as a Little-Mirrlees shadow price.

Alternatively, one may take a less policy activist view of the adjustment process. Let's pretend that fully flexible wages and the real balance effect keep the economy's labor force fully employed and the balance of payments in equilibrium. Here we have substituted effective market mechanisms for policy activism. In this case, the shadow price of foreign exchange would show the increased real income that would result from the government either giving one unit of foreign exchange to the private sector or trading one unit of foreign exchange to the private sector in return for one unit of domestic currency, where this increased real income is what results after the real balance effect and the wage flexibility have restored equilibrium in both the labor and foreign exchange markets. Similarly, the shadow price of labor shows how much foreign exchange the government would have to release from reserves each period if it were to withdraw one unit of labor from the private sector and wished to leave real income unchanged, after the adjustment mechanisms worked themselves out.[1] Finally, to find the effect on real income of releasing one unit of labor previously employed by the government to the private sector,

---

[1]Sieper (1981) views the shadow prices of non-traded goods in the same way.

assuming that the government leaves its foreign exchange reserves unchanged one would just multiply the shadow price of labor (Δ in foreign exchange saved/Δ in labor supplied) by the shadow price of foreign exchange, [Δy/Δ in foreign exchange spent] to get Δy/[Δ in labor supplied], the shadow price of labor in utility numeraire, i.e. in domestic real income numeraire.

3.   Shadow Pricing Labor

Labor can be consumed directly as massages or else used in combination with a fixed factor and an intermediate input to produce widgets. Widgets and their intermediate inputs are traded internationally at a fixed world price and the representative domestic consumer consumes both labor services and widgets with the ratio depending on the price of widgets relative to labor services. There are no distortions associated with the production or consumption of massages, but there is an export subsidy on widgets.

Figures 3a-d describe what happens when a compensated appreciation of the country's currency (the peso) occurs.[1] Figure 3a shows the production possibility frontier (PPF) for widgets and labor services consumed by the private sector under the assumption that the labor absorbed by the government is fixed. Production is initially at x^o. Also in (3a) the economy is shown to be consuming initially at c^o on indifference curve I. c^o and x^o have the same height indicating that all massages are consumed by the private sector, but c^o lies to the left of x^o indicating that some widgets are produced for export and that some are sold to the government for use in projects.

In figure 3b the ray OC shows the cost in foreign exchange (dollars) of varying levels of widget consumption. Its slope, p*, represents the world price of widgets. The ray OX shows value added in widget production measured at world prices. I.e., it shows the dollar value of widgets produced minus the dollar value of plastic used up in their production. Consequently its slope is given by $p^* - a\pi^* = v^*$ where a is the number of units of plastic used up in the production of a widget, π^* is the dollar price of plastic and v^* is unit value added at world prices. Given consumption at C^o and production at X^o, the economy is initially producing FX^o dollars worth of widgets net of plastic inputs and consuming FC^o dollars worth of widgets, which leaves $F^o = FX^o - FC^o$ dollars for the government to spend on projects or for it to add to its foreign currency reserves each period.

We define one unit of labor services as that which trades for one peso. This means that we can plot the slope of I (with positive sign) in 3c, which then represents the compensated demand curve for widgets, with pesos/widget or labor/widget on the vertical axis. This also means that we can plot the slope of the PPF (again with positive sign) in 3c which then represents the supply of value added in widget production with unit value added measured in pesos on the vertical axis. The economy is shown to be initially consuming C^o widgets with a peso price of widgets of p^o and producing X^o widgets with unit value added measured in pesos of v^o.

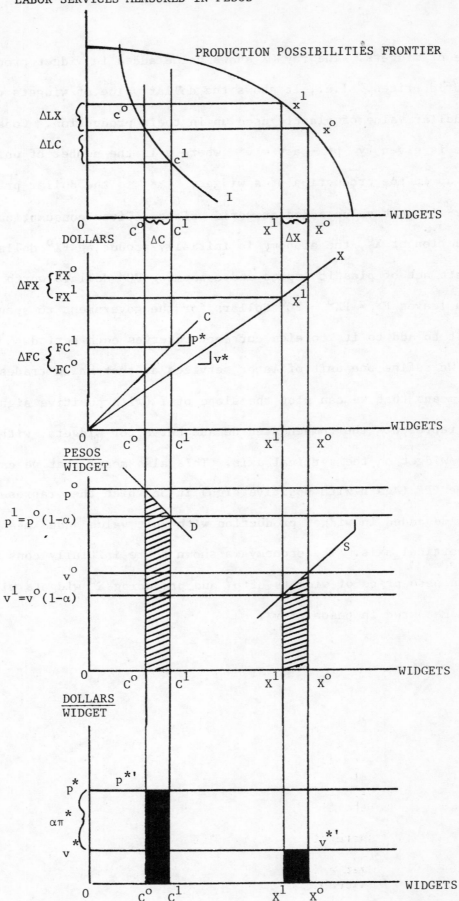

LABOR SERVICES MEASURED IN PESOS

PRODUCTION POSSIBILITIES FRONTIER

Figure 3a

Figure 3b

Figure 3c

Figure 3d

37

In figure 3d the slopes of OC and OX from figure 3b are plotted. We can use that figure to see that initially $0v*v*'X^o$ dollars are being earned in the process of adding value in widgets while $0p*p*'C^o$ dollars worth of widgets are being consumed.

Now let us consider what happens when the peso is appreciated by a (small) proportion α and tax policy keeps consumers on the same indifference curve. The peso price of widgets falls to $p^1 = p^o(1-\alpha)$. This raises widget consumption to C^1 and cuts the consumption of labor services by ΔLC in 3a, which is equal to the striped area under D in 3c. However, the increased widget consumption bears a foreign exchange cost equal to ΔFC in 3b which is equal to the shaded area between C^1 and C^o in 3d. Denoting the elasticity of the compensated demand curve for widgets as η (defined to be positive) the increased consumption of widgets is given by $\Delta C = \eta C^o \alpha$. This means that to the first approximation $p^o \eta C^o \alpha$ units of labor have been released from the production of labor services while $p* \eta C^o \alpha$ dollars more as being spent on the consumption of widgets.

The appreciation of the peso causes unit value added in pesos to fall from v^o to $v^1 = v^o(1-\alpha)$ in 3c. This means that widget production will fall from X^o to X^1, where we can write $\Delta X = X^o - X^1 = eX^o \alpha$ where e is the elasticity of supply of widgets with respect to the price of value added, i.e. unit value added.[1] This results in a release of labor from widget production

---

[1] It makes intuitive sense that this elasticity should be identical to the elasticity of output with respect to the wage rate, since labor is the only non-fixed factor used in the production of value added. This is demonstrated in Tower (1984, section V.9a). Also, just following equation (6') of Tower (1984, section II.2) it is demonstrated that this elasticity is given by $e = \sigma \theta_L / \theta_K$ where σ is the elasticity of substitution between capital and labor

and θ_L / θ_K is the share of labor relative to that of capital in the production of value added. Over a fairly short time horizon values of $\sigma = 1/3$ and θ_L / θ_K of 3/1 might be reasonable giving a value of 1 for e.

equal to ΔLX in 3a, which is equal to the striped area under S in 3c, and is given to a first approximation by $v^o e X^o \alpha$. The foreign exchange cost of the labor released is given by ΔFX in 3b, which is equal to the shaded area between X^1 and X^o in 3d, $v*eX^o \alpha$.

The ratio of increased foreign exchange expenditure to labor released is given by

$$c_\ell = \frac{\Delta F}{\Delta L} = \frac{\Delta FC + \Delta FX}{\Delta LC + \Delta LX} = \frac{p* \Delta C + v* \Delta X}{p \Delta C + v \Delta X} = \frac{p* \eta^o C \alpha + v* e X^o \alpha}{p \eta C^o \alpha + v e X^o \alpha} = \frac{p* \eta C^o + v* e X^o}{p \eta C^o + v e X^o}$$

where SPL is the shadow price of labor and c_ℓ is the conversion factor for labor. The conversion factor for a good or factor is the cost in foreign exchange of an amount of a good or factor valued at one unit of domestic currency, and the shadow price of a good or factor is the cost in foreign exchange of one unit of the good or factor. Since the wage is normalized at unity, c_ℓ is both the conversion factor for labor and its shadow price.

If we define one unit of foreign exchange as the amount of foreign currency which initially sells for one peso, which is referred to in the literature as a "border peso," then we can write $p^o = (1+\tau)p*$ where τ is the export subsidy on widgets expressed as a fraction of the world price. Moreover, using this definition we can write $v = (1 + ERP)v*$ where ERP is the effective rate of protection, which is defined as the proportion by which v exceeds $v*$. Combining these last three relationships gives

$$c_\ell = \frac{\text{Foreign Exchange Saved}}{\text{Value of Labor Used}} = \frac{\eta p* C^o + e v*^o X^o}{(1+\tau) \eta p* C^o + (1+ERP) e v*^o X^o}. \tag{1}$$

Now let us introduce two complications. First, let's suppose there is a value added tax at a rate VAT in widgets.[1] In this case the wage bill paid out to incremental primary factors of production (in this case labor), from the employer's perspective is still the striped area in 3c but only a fraction (1-VAT) of that is actually received by workers. Secondly, let's now assume that widget labor is paid a premium of b over the wage elsewhere, so the opportunity cost of the labor absorbed by widgets is only a fraction 1/(1+b) of the wages received by incremental workers in widgets. Combining these three terms we see that the value of labor (measured at wages in the services sector) absorbed into widgets is

$$\Delta LX = \frac{(1-VAT)ev^{o}X^{o}\alpha}{(1+b)}.$$

Thus we can rewrite c_ℓ as

$$c_\ell = \frac{\eta p^{*o}C^{o}+ev^{*o}X^{o}}{(1+\tau)\eta p^{*o}C^{o}+ (1+z)ev^{*o}X^{o}} \tag{2}$$

where

$$z = (1+ERP)(1-VAT)/(1+b) - 1$$

and z can be thought of as the implicit rate of value-added subsidy in widget production. Dropping the zero superscripts

$$c_\ell = 1 - \frac{\tau\eta E^{*} + zeV^{*}}{(1+\tau)\eta C^{*} + (1+z)eV^{*}} \tag{3}$$

---

[1]We assume that the value added tax is on widget production only and not on massages.

where $V^* = v^*X$ is total value added in widget production, valued at world prices and $C^* = p^*C$ is consumption of widgets valued at world prices. Thus we see that the market overvalues labor to the extent that τ and ERP are positive, and undervalues labor to the extent that b and VAT are positive.

Why is this so? When the government withdraws labor for a project, internal balance dictates appreciation of the currency in order to release the requisite labor from the two sectors. This appreciation will expand consumption of the artificially expensive widgets and reduce production of the implicitly subsidized widgets, where the implicit degree of subsidization depends positively on ERP and negatively on both b and VAT. Assuming both τ and z are positive, both the expanded widget consumption and contracted widget production are welfare increasing, and are reflected in the conversion factor for labor being less than unity, i.e., in the shadow price of labor being less than its market price.

4. Many Commodities, Some of Which are Imported and Some of Which are Exported

We have pretended that the domestic economy produces and consumes only two goods. However, we can imagine that the economy produces many goods. If each is traded at fixed world prices and uses intermediate inputs which are also traded at fixed world prices along with labor plus a fixed sector-specific capital stock, and if domestic consumption of each good depends solely on its price relative to that of labor services, (3) becomes

$$c_\ell = 1 - \frac{\sum\limits_i \left[\tau_i \eta_i C_i^* + z_i e_i V_i^* \right]}{\sum\limits_i \left[(1+\tau_i) \eta_i C_i^* + (1+z_i) e_i V_i^* \right]} \qquad (4)$$

where $z_i = (1+ERP_i)(1-VAT_i)/(1+b_i) - 1$

and the i subscript refers to the ith good so that VAT_i is the value added tax on the ith good etc. Finally, to account for imports as well as exports we need only redefine τ_i as the proportion by which the domestic price of i exceeds the world price, i.e. the ad valorem import tariff or export subsidy expressed as a proportion of the world price.

5. Non-Standard Adjustment Mechanisms

Suppose that exchange rate change and wage flexibility are ruled out as adjustment mechanisms because of a commitment to a fixed exchange rate combined with inflexibility of nominal wages. Furthermore, let us suppose that the adjustment mechanism used is a proportional change in the force of each import tariff, export subsidy or implicit value added subsidy (z) given by

$$d\tau_i/(1 + \tau_i) = \beta_i$$

and

$$dz_i/(1 + z_i) = \gamma_i.$$

In this case it is easy to show that due to the adjustment on the demand side the increase in labor demanded in the labor services sector is given by

$\sum_i p_i \eta_i C_i \beta_i$ while the foreign exchange saved is $-\sum_i p_i^* \Delta C_i = \sum_i p_i^* \eta_i C_i \beta_i$. On the

supply side these two figures are $\sum_i e_i v_i X_i \gamma_i$ and $\sum_i e_i v_i^* X_i \gamma_i$ so our new

expression for the shadow price of labor becomes

$$c_\ell = 1 - \frac{\sum_i [\tau_i \eta_i C_i^* \beta_i + z_i e_i V_i^* \gamma_i]}{\sum_i [(1+\tau_i)\eta_i C_i^* \beta_i + (1+z_i)e_i V_i^* \gamma_i]} . \tag{5}$$

Note, that in certain cases this will generate very simple formulae. For example if the authorities alter only the consumption tax on the nth good, since τ_n is defined as $(p_n/p_n^*) - 1$, production of all goods will be unchanged as will consumption of all goods but the nth. This yields $\alpha_n \neq 0$ but all other αs and βs will be zero. Thus we have

$$c_\ell = 1 - \frac{\tau_n}{(1+\tau_n)} = \frac{1}{1+\tau_n} . \tag{6}$$

Similarly if only the effective rate of protection of the nth good is changed due to a judicious juggling of tariffs on inputs

$$c_\ell = 1 - \frac{z_n}{1 + z_n} = \frac{1}{1 + z_n} . \tag{7}$$

6. Proving that the Conversion Factor For Converting Domestic Real Income into Foreign Exchange is The Sum of The Shadow Prices of Goods Each Weighted By the Marginal Propensity To Consume It

Scott (1974) notes that the conversion factor for converting domestic real income into foreign exchange is the sum of the shadow prices of goods each weighted by the marginal propensity to consume it, although he does not prove that this is the case. However, it is quite easy to see that the proposition must hold. Suppose that the government endows our representative consumer with a basket of goods, with the quantity of each good in the basket, $\bar{Q}_i$, given by the marginal propensity to consume it at constant prices: $\bar{Q}_i = m_i^* = m_i/p_i$ where m_i^* is the marginal propensity to consume good i out of real income, m_i is the marginal propensity to spend on good i out of real income, y, and p_i is the price of good i to our representative consumer. Since $\sum_i m_i = 1$, $dy = \sum_i p_i \bar{Q}_i = \Sigma m_i = 1$, which is to say, the initial effect is to change his real income by unity, and since he has been endowed with extra goods in the proportions in which he naturally spends increments to his income at constant prices, no excess demands or supplies will develop. Therefore, the ultimate effect is no different from the initial effect. Now suppose that instead of endowing the individual with this basket, the government endows the economy with an additional amount of foreign exchange, $\bar{F}$, which is equal to the shadow price of the basket: $\bar{F} = \sum_i SP_i m_i^*$, where SP_i is the shadow price of the ith good. By the definition of shadow price, this quantity of foreign exchange must generate the same real income as the basket itself. Let us define the conversion factor for real income, c_y, as the extra amount of foreign exchange needed to increase real income by one unit. This gives us

$$dy = 1 = \bar{F}/c_y = \sum_i SP_i m_i^*/c_y \text{ or } c_y = \sum_i SP_i m_i^*.$$

Thus we see that the conversion factor is the sum of the shadow prices of the goods weighted by the marginal propensities to spend as Scott (1974) indicates.

7. Calculating the Shadow Price of Foreign Exchange

From the above argument we can rewrite the conversion factor for real income, c_y, as

$$c_y = \sum_i SP_i(m_i/p_i) = \sum m_i(SP_i/p_i) = \Sigma \, m_i c_i \qquad (8)$$

where SP_i is the shadow price of good i, c_i is its conversion factor and m_i is the marginal propensity to spend on the ith good with $\sum m_i = 1$. Also c_y is the foreign exchange used, $\bar{F}$, to increase real income, y, by one unit, so

$$\bar{F} = c_y dy. \qquad (9)$$

Now, we define the shadow price of foreign exchange in utility numeraire, SPFX, as the amount of real income which would have to be sacrificed in order to earn one unit of foreign exchange. This means that

$$SPFX = dy/\bar{F} = 1/c_y = 1/\sum_i m_i c_i. \qquad (10)$$

In our models, as for Little and Mirrlees (1974), the conversion factor for each of the traded goods is simply the ratio of border price to consumer price or $1/(1+\tau_i)$, while the conversion factor for our non-traded good and mobile factor labor is c_ℓ from (2), (3), (4), (5), (6) or (7). This means that we can write the shadow price of foreign exchange as

$$SPFX = 1/\left[\sum_i m_i/(1+\tau_i) + m_\ell c_\ell\right] \qquad (11)$$

where m_ℓ is the marginal propensity to spend on labor services and i is an index that runs over traded goods only. Note that in the special case where all $m_i = 0$ so $m_\ell = 1$, the shadow price of foreign exchange is given by the reciprocal of the conversion factor for labor.

This relationship between the shadow price of foreign exchange and the shadow prices of goods is quite a useful one. For one thing, it emphasizes that the shadow price of foreign exchange will depend on the structure of marginal propensities to consume by those who are directly affected by the tax or subsidy which converts real income into foreign exchange, and the shadow price of foreign exchange will alter when the government switches from a system of direct taxes which affects one group of consumers to an alternative which primarily effects other consumers with different marginal propensities to consume. Moreover, the analysis clarifies a point made by Balassa (1974, pp. 161-162) who writes:

> The shadow exchange rate will also have to be used to value commodities whose prices and domestic consumption are affected by the implementation of the project. This will be the case if the project produces or uses nontraded goods supplied at nonconstant costs, commodities subject to quotas or prohibitive tariffs, or export products facing less than infinitely elastic world demand. In such instances, consumer-producer surplus analysis needs to be made in domestic values and the shadow exchange rate used to convert domestic values into world market prices or vice versa.

> . . .

> In cases when not all products are fully traded, estimating the social opportunity cost of primary factors, as well as valuing commodities

whose prices and domestic consumption are affected by the project will require using the shadow exchange rate as conversion factor.

Thus Balassa seems to be arguing that the shadow exchange rate should be used to convert both domestic real income (producer and consumer surplus) into foreign exchange and to shadow price domestic non-traded goods and factors of production, where foreign exchange is the numeraire.

However, as we have seen this is valid only when the marginal propensity to spend on our non-traded good is unity and the corresponding marginal propensity for all other goods is zero. That this must be true in this case is obvious, because in this case increasing the private sector's real income by one unit of domestic currency will result in withdrawal of labor services worth precisely that amount from other uses,[1] and the cost of this in foreign exchange is precisely the conversion factor for labor.

---

[1] Incidentally, it should be noted that the formula we present in (2) is identical to the reciprocal of Balassa's (1974) formula for the shadow price of foreign exchange when there are no intermediate inputs, no distortions except taxes and subsidies on trade, and summation signs are used to indicate many goods.

8. Integrating Our Results With Those of Bacha-Taylor (1971)

Bacha-Taylor (1971, p. 206) present a formula for the shadow price of foreign exchange in utility numeraire that seems at first glance to conflict with ours. They write (p. 204) what they call the Harberger-Schydlowsky-Fontaine (HSF) formula for the shadow price of foreign exchange as

$$HSF_1 = \frac{\sum_i (1+\tau_i) p_i^* dM_i}{\sum p_i^* dM_i} \qquad (12)^1$$

where τ_i is the ad valorem import tariff or export subsidy on good i and dM_i is the change in net imports. This follows from the facts that with fixed world prices and no domestic distortions, foreign exchange used can be written as

$$\bar{F} = \sum_i p_i^* dM_i \qquad (13)$$

and

$$dy = \sum_i p_i^*(1+\tau_i) dM_i \qquad (14)$$

so that

$$HSF_1 = \frac{dy}{\bar{F}} = \frac{\sum_i p_i^*(1+\tau_i) dM_i}{\sum_i p_i^* dM_i} . \qquad (15)$$

On p. 206 this formula is rewritten as

$$HSF_2 = \frac{\sum_i (1+t_i) \mu_i \eta_i}{\sum_i \mu_i \eta_i} \qquad (16)$$

---

[1]We have modified their expression to streamline it and have used our own notation.

48

where η_i is the domestic elasticity of excess demand for the ith traded good with respect to the exchange rate and μ_i is the share of net imports of sector i in total imports.[1] Note that (16) follows from (15) so long as μ_i is defined as $p_i^*/M_i / \sum_i | p_i^* M_i |$ and $\eta_i = -\hat{M}_i/\hat{r}$.

Equation (16) involves only elasticities whereas our equation (11) involves marginal propensities to spend. Doesn't this mean that one of these equations is wrong?

The answer is no. It is only necessary to remember that the Bacha–Taylor η_i is not a compensated price elasticity of excess demand. Rather it is a general equilibrium elasticity of excess demand with respect to the exchange rate. Moreover to solve for this elasticity one must postulate an adjustment mechanism which keeps the demand for labor just equal to its exogenously given supply. Finally, any adjustment mechanism may be postulated. For example each 1% fall in the price of domestic currency might be accompanied by increases in certain export taxes to mitigate the resulting inflation. The only problem is that the numerical value of the elasticity will depend on the adjustment mechanism assumed. Thus the Bacha–Taylor η's when correctly calculated will incorporate our m's, and if tariffs and effective tariffs are also changing they will incorporate our β's and γ's as well.

One may rightly ask how useful this Bacha–Taylor formula is since it presupposes having built and differentiated a general equilibrium model. Still, there is one special case where the Bacha–Taylor η turns out to be simply the price elasticity of compensated excess demand. That is in the

---

[1] Both Bacha–Taylor and Balassa (1974) work with imports and exports separately, but for convenience we have lumped them together and therefore need only deal with the concept of net imports.

model we built first in this chapter, where intermediate inputs and all distortions except for taxes and subsidies on trade are assumed away when we also assume that the marginal propensity to spend on labor services is unity and the marginal propensity to spend on all other goods is zero.[1]

---

[1]The same point applies to Balassa's (1974) formula for the shadow price of foreign exchange. He does not tell us precisely how his demand elasticity η_m is defined. If it is a compensated demand elasticity his formula always shadow prices labor correctly and when $m_\ell = 1$ and $m_i = 0$ it correctly shadow prices utility. However, if we interpret η_m as a general equilibrium elasticity of demand holding labor use constant but allowing real income, y, to vary his same formula but with a different meaning attached to η_m also correctly shadow prices foreign exchange in utility numeraire as well.

Chapter III

HOW TO USE SOME SHADOW PRICES TO FIND OTHERS:

Tricks for Lazy People Who Don't Like

Solving General Equilibrium Systems

1. Introduction

In this chapter, we first show in what sense it is true that the shadow price of a factor of production can be expressed as the sum of its marginal net products with each evaluated at its shadow price. Next we show how a nontraded good or a good whose world price is variable can be shadow priced in terms of the shadow prices of other goods.

Then, we show that policy parameters, e.g. taxes, subsidies, tariffs and quotas as well as exogenous parameters like foreign prices and technological changes can also be shadow priced in terms of goods in a very similar way. Our treatment consists of a discussion of the essential logic underlying the solution of these problems, followed by analysis of some special cases which express our solutions in terms of conversion factors of various sorts. Finally, we show how recognizing the heterogeneity of individual consuming units complicates the problem of shadow pricing one item in terms of others, but still leaves it tractable.

2. Shadow Pricing a Factor of Production as the Sum of Its Marginal Net Products with Each Valued at Its Shadow Price

A number of authors have argued that the shadow price of a factor of production can be expressed as the sum of its marginal net products, with each weighted by its shadow price. For example Little-Mirrlees (1974, p. 169-174) note that the shadow wage rate is equal to the sum of the marginal products of labor in the activities from which it is withdrawn each valued at its shadow price if we assume that no additional consumption is generated by the new employment. Let us now make this notion more precise, prove that it holds and tie it in with the concept of the effective rate of protection.

First consider a country where there are N factors of production which produce N goods, all of which are traded at fixed world prices and have fixed tariffs attached but no quantitative restrictions, so that domestic prices are fixed. This means that both output levels and input prices will be determinate. When the government releases one unit of a factor of production into the economy some outputs will rise and some may fall, as in Srinivason-Bhagwati (1978) and Srinivason (1982), but no prices of either outputs or factors of production will alter. Hence factor wages and goods prices will all remain unchanged, so that (assuming the government was initially paying a competitive wage to the factor of production it released) private sector real income and consumption of every good will also be unchanged. The only effect will be that net exports of each good will rise by the incremental net output of each good, earning for the government an amount of foreign exchange equal to the sum of the net increases in output of the various goods valued at their world prices, i.e., their Little-Mirrlees shadow prices. Since the Little-Mirrlees shadow price of an item is defined as the amount of foreign exchange which the government can extract upon releasing one unit of the item into the private sector without altering private sector real income we have demonstrated a special case of the proposition cited above.

Now consider a slightly more complex model. There are still N primary factors and N goods, but some or all of them are non-traded. Now pretend that the goverment freezes all output prices by buying or selling the goods on demand so as to match any change in the private sector's excess supply or demand. The government releases one unit of one factor and acquires all changes in net outputs. Since no incomes or prices have altered, both private sector real incomes and consumptions of all goods including leisure must be the same. Thus private sector real income is unchanged by the release of the factor and simultaneous official absorption of the goods. This means that the shadow price of the labor released must be just equal to the value at shadow prices of the goods absorbed, and again our proposition holds.

Finally, pretend that the numbers of goods and factors are not necessarily the same, and the government releases one unit of one factor of production while absorbing increased net outputs at constant prices. If the number of goods exceeds the number of factors, output levels will depend on which bundle of goods the government buys while factor prices will be frozen. Still, our proposition will hold regardless of which bundle of goods the government stimulates production of by expanded net purchases.

If the number of factors exceeds the number of goods, output levels will be determined solely by factor supplies and goods prices but factor prices and real incomes will depend on factor supplies, which invalidates our proposition. To restore it, we must assume that the government compensates the private sector by adjusting the income tax or subsidy rates on each factor so that after tax factor incomes are unchanged.[1] Once this is done private sector real incomes and consumption levels will be restored to their initial

---

[1]If factors are in inelastic supply and there is no problem in aggregating households because a social welfare function exists as rationalized in one of the ways discussed in Tower (1979), then all we need to do is adjust the income tax so as to freeze total factor income to the whole economy.

values, and again our proposition holds. This all leads to the following conclusion.

The shadow price of a factor of production is equal to the sum of its marginal net products, each valued at its shadow price, where the marginal net products are calculated under the assumption that the government releases a unit of the factor of production and adjusts its purchases and sales of goods so as to freeze their prices, while simultaneously adjusting factor specific income taxes and subsidies so as to leave after tax wage rates unchanged. Finally, this proposition holds quite generally. For example production functions need not be first degree homogeneous, factors need not be inelastically supplied, and utility functions need not be independent.

Now let's reckon with the interindustry structure of production. Suppose that the government's release of the factor causes the widget sector to expand, which involves increased use of plastic. Then the factor's marginal net product in widgets is positive and in plastic it is negative. Alternatively, let's pretend that plastic is used in fixed proportions to produce widgets. Then we can think of the widget sector as producing a basket of two goods: widgets in positive quantities and plastic in negative quantities. Unit value added at shadow prices is just the price of one such basket, containing plus one widget and minus the plastic needed to produce it.[1] In this alternative framework we can think of the marginal net product of labor in this sector as the extra number of baskets produced, and if all goods are traded at fixed world prices, the shadow price of each basket would simply be value added at world prices, and the conversion factor for the basket (the ratio of the basket's shadow value to market value) would simply

---

[1] For more on this way of thinking about value added see Tower (1984, ch. IV).

be 1/[1+ERP], where ERP is the effective rate of protection. More generally, it would be 1/[1+ERPSP] where ERPSP is the proportional difference between unit value added at domestic prices and at shadow prices.

Finally, it is possible to couch all of our analysis in terms of a conversion factor. If a factor is paid the value of its marginal product, when the government releases a unit of the factor to the private sector, the sum of the marginal net products evaluated at market prices will equal the value of the factor released. Then since the shadow price of the factor is equal to the shadow price of its marginal net product vector, the conversion factor for labor, i.e. the ratio of its shadow price to its market value will equal the conversion factor for the vector of marginal net products of labor, i.e. its shadow value divided by its market value.

3. Shadow Pricing Goods in Terms of the Shadow Prices of Other Goods and Shadow Pricing Policy and Non-Policy Parameters in Terms of the Shadow Prices of Goods

Suppose that we have already solved a general equilibrium model, so that we have shadow prices for goods and factors at some level of aggregation. But now suppose that we wish to evaluate a project which uses or produces either a new good or else a narrowly defined good which we have not previously shadow priced, and is not traded at fixed world prices, so it is difficult to shadow price.

To shadow price this good, which we call the 0th good, we perform the following conceptual experiment. Suppose the government meets all of the demand forthcoming at some price incrementally below the market clearing price which would prevail in the absence of government sales. Suppose also that the government pegs the prices of all other goods by offering to buy or sell unlimited quantities at their initial market prices while keeping the economy's real income at its initial level through adjustments in some sort of tax, which need not be non-distorting.

The change in the real income of the private sector is by definition the sum of the increases in the excess supplies of the various goods by the government (where foreign exchange is one of the goods) with each evaluated at its Little-Mirrlees shadow price[1], all times the shadow price of foreign exchange in utility numeraire. But this change is zero. Thus, the shadow price of the quantity of the 0th good supplied by the government must be equal to the shadow price of the bundle of other goods (including foreign exchange) bought by the government. Therefore we can shadow price the 0th good as

$$SP_0 = - \sum_{i \neq 0} \frac{\partial ED_i}{\partial \overline{Q}_0} \cdot SP_i \qquad (1)$$

where SP_i is the shadow price of the ith good, $\overline{Q}_0$ is the autonomous change in the quantity of the 0'th good supplied by the government, ED_i is the private economy's excess demand for good i, $\partial ED_i / \partial \overline{Q}_0$ is the change in the private sector's excess demand for good i per unit of good 0 supplied by the government, holding domestic private sector real income and the prices of all goods except good 0 constant, and the index i runs over all goods except good 0. The term ED_i can be broken down into the consumption demand by the domestic private sector minus the domestic private sector's supply plus the

---

[1] A Little-Mirrlees shadow price is a shadow price expressed in foreign exchange numeraire. For a discussion of its relationship to the alternative UNIDO shadow pricing technique which involves expressing shadow prices in utility or real income numeraire, but which is not discussed in this paper (although that is how we shadow price foreign exchange) see chapter 2 of Tower (1984).

excess demand by the foreign sector. In subsequent sections (III.5 - III.8) of this chapter we draw implications of this breakdown.

Now let us consider the effects of an infinitesimal change of some parameter, $d\overline{P}$, be it either a policy parameter like a tariff or a quota or a non-policy parameter like technology, foreign excess demand, or world price. We define the (Little-Mirrlees) shadow price of a parameter as the amount of foreign exchange which the government can absorb in conjunction with a unit increase in the parameter and still leave private sector real income unchanged. For this conceptual experiment we assume that the government holds all goods prices fixed at their initial market clearing levels by being willing to supply or demand unlimited quantities, and again, pretend that it pegs real income by varying some sort of not necessarily non-distorting tax. The change in real income is by definition the sum of the changes in official excess supplies of the various goods plus the change in the parameter, all evaluated at their Little-Mirrlees shadow prices and multiplied by the shadow price of foreign exchange in utility numeraire. Since real income has not changed, the shadow price of a change in the policy parameter must be just equal to minus the sum of the changes in the private sector's excess demands for the various goods (where again foreign exchange is one of the goods) each evaluated at its shadow price. Thus we can write the shadow price of this parameter change as

$$SPd\overline{P} = -d\overline{P} \sum_i SP_i \, \partial ED_i / \partial \overline{P} \qquad (2)$$

where i runs over all goods and $\partial ED_i / \partial \overline{P}$ is the change in the private sector's excess demand for the ith good with respect to a unit change in the parameter holding all goods prices and real income constant. In subsequent sections of this chapter (III.6 and III.7) we rewrite this expression and draw implications.

4. Shadow Pricing a Good or Factor in Terms of Other Goods and Factors

It is possible to generalize some of the results of the preceding two sections as follows. Suppose there are G goods, N factors of production, no joint products, constant returns to scale and perfect competition. Then if we know the prices for any set of N items, be they goods, factors or some combination of the two, we can solve the G relationships between factor prices and goods prices for the remaining G prices. With prices given, factor proportions can now be determined. Then if we are given any G outputs, factor supplies or combination of the two, we can solve the N factor demand equations for the remaining N factor supplies, outputs or combination of the two.

Thus if the government pegs the prices of N items and the quantities of G items, all N + G prices will be invariant with respect to any changes in the pegged quantities. Also, all quantities will be determinate, meaning that all shadow prices will be determinate (see Bertrand [1979]). This means that if we wish to shadow price the 0th item (be it a factor or good) in terms of N other items (be they factors, goods or some combination), we can imagine the government to peg the prices of these N items by satisfying any excess demands at initial market prices. Then when the government injects one unit of the 0th item into the economy it notes the excess supplies of the N items which develop at constant prices, and the shadow price of the 0th item can be calculated as the value of the excess supplies of the other items when evaluated at their shadow prices.

Thus, if we have just as many factors of production as we have traded goods it will always be possible to shadow price all of the factors of production and hence all goods in terms of the set of traded goods. Moreover,

it will frequently be worthwhile to specify a shadow pricing model so that it
has this property in order to be tractable.

5. Using Demand Side and Supply Side Conversion Factors to Shadow Price a
    Non-Traded Good

Squire and van der Tak (1975, pp. 144-145) and Ray (1984, ch. 5) both
recommend shadow pricing a non-traded good as a weighted average of a supply
side and a demand side conversion factor where the weights depend on the
elasticities of demand for and supply of the non-traded good in question.
However, they don't explain why this is a legitimate procedure, or precisely
how to define the demand and supply elasticities or the demand and supply side
conversion factors, and it appears that the formulae are valid only when
quantities demanded and supplied of all other non-traded goods are fixed in
response to a small change in the government's excess demand for the non-
traded good.

In this section we use results from sections II.6, III.2 and III.3 to
demonstrate that the Squire-van der Tak-Ray formulae are legitimate even when
expenditure is shifted onto other non-traded goods by government purchase of a
unit of the particular non-traded good, and we define precisely what is meant
by the two conversion factors. Then in section III.6 we define a foreign
market conversion factor and show that it enables us to shadow price in a
still more general model where foreign excess demands and supplies for traded
commodities are interrelated.

Let us consider a closed economy, i.e. one where there is no foreign
trade. p_i^c and p_i^p are the prices of the ith good to consumers and producers.
These two prices are assumed to be linked by a constant ad valorem excise tax

or subsidy, so $\hat{p}_i^c = \hat{p}_i^p$ where a "^" denotes a proportional change. In what follows we denote this common proportional change simply as $\hat{p}_i$. Suppose the government offers to buy unlimited quantities of the 0th commodity at some price incrementally greater than the initial market clearing price and at the same time it pegs the prices of all other commodities at their initial market clearing prices by standing ready to buy and sell unlimited quantities, while leaving real income unchanged by adjusting non-distorting lump sum tax rates. Clearly, since real income has not changed, the shadow price of the quantity of the 0th good which the government purchased, must be equal to the shadow price of the basket of all the goods which the government supplies net to the private sector as a consequence of its purchases of good 0. The amount of the 0th good acquired by the government, $-\overline{Q}_0$, is $[\eta_0 C_0 + e_0 X_0]\hat{p}_0$ where C_0 and X_0 are respectively the initial levels of demand and supply, $\eta_i > 0$ is the compensated demand elasticity for good i and e_i is the supply elasticity of good i holding all other output prices constant.

The quantity of the ith good which the government must supply in return is given by $\hat{p}_0 [C_i \eta_{i0} - X_i e_{i0}]$ where C_i and X_i are respectively consumption demand and supply for i and η_{i0} and e_{i0} are respectively the compensated crossprice elasticity of demand and crossprice elasticity of supply of good i with respect to good 0's price.

Equating the shadow value of the good 0 absorbed to the shadow value of the bundle supplied by the government yields

$$SP_0 = \frac{\hat{p}_0 \sum_{i \neq 0} [C_i \eta_{i0} - X_i e_{i0}] SP_i}{[\eta_0 C_0 + e_0 X_0]\hat{p}_0} . \tag{3}$$

We define the demand side conversion factor for good 0, c_{d0}, as the ratio of the incremental consumption bundle containing all goods other than 0 valued at shadow prices to the reduced consumption of the 0th commodity valued at its consumer price, p_0^c. Thus,

$$c_{d0} = \frac{\sum\limits_{i \neq 0} SP_i C_i \eta_{i0} \hat{P}_0}{p_0^c \eta_0 C_0 \hat{P}_0} = \frac{\sum\limits_{i \neq 0} SP_i C_i \eta_{i0}}{p_0^c \eta_0 C_0} \ . \tag{4}$$

But since along a compensated demand curve $\Sigma \, p_i^c dC_i = 0$ we have alternatively

$$c_{d0} = \frac{\sum\limits_{i \neq 0} SP_i C_i \eta_{i0}}{\sum\limits_{i \neq 0} p_i^c C_i \eta_{i0}} \tag{5}$$

i.e., the ratio of the value of the incremental consumption bundle at shadow prices divided by the value of the same bundle at consumer prices.

Similarly, the supply side converstion factor for good 0, c_{s0}, is defined as the ratio of the incremental reduction of the output basket of all goods other than 0 evaluated at shadow prices to the increase of output of the 0th commodity evaluated at its producer price. Thus

$$c_{s0} = - \frac{\sum\limits_{i \neq 0} SP_i X_i e_{i0}}{p_0^p e_0 X_0} \ . \tag{6}$$

Assuming that factors are paid their marginal products, the value at producers' prices of increased production of 0 will equal the value of the factors absorbed into 0 production, and this will equal the value at producers' prices of reduced production of other goods. Thus, the denominator of (6) can equally well be written as the reduction in the output of other goods evaluated at producer prices, p_i^p, so

$$c_{s0} = \frac{\sum\limits_{i \neq 0} SP_i X_i e_{i0}}{\sum\limits_{i \neq 0} p_i^p X_i \, e_{i0}} \ . \tag{7}$$

61

So the supply side conversion factor can be expressed as the ratio of the value at shadow prices to the value at producer prices of the incremental production bundle of "other" goods. It should be noted that in this thought experiment, factor prices may be altering, so that e_{i0} is a general equilibrium elasticity which reckons with any factor price changes generated by the change in p_0^p . Plugging (4) and (6) into (3) yields

$$SP_0 = \frac{p_0^c \eta_0 C_0 c_{d0} + p_0^p e_0 X_0 c_{s0}}{\eta_0 C_0 + e_0 X_0} . \tag{8}$$

How might this formula be useful? If good 0 is narrowly defined, and we have shadow prices for broad aggregates consisting of i = 1, ..., N which we have derived from a general equilibrium model, this formula enables us to shadow price good 0 without having to go back to insert more detail into our general equilibrium calculation. Similarly, if good 0 is a new good not previously shadow priced, the formula will enable us to shadow price it.

We have described one conceptual experiment for shadow pricing one good in terms of others. But, in fact, other frameworks are feasible as well. Suppose the government again uses purchases to raise p_0 incrementally, while simultaneously pegging other commodity prices at their initial levels by supplying them on demand, but this time it pegs the price of intersectorally mobile factors by supplying them on demand. In that case, it will need to supply commodities only to meet the increased consumption and to supply only the incremental factor bundle which is absorbed into sector 0, and again the shadow price of the good 0 withdrawn will equal the shadow price of the bundle of factors and other goods supplied. Note that if the prices of intersectorally mobile factors would have changed in the previous conceptual experiment, then the supply elasticities for good 0 in the two conceptual experiments must be different. Otherwise, they will be the same, and where they are the same, the shadow price of the mobile factors drawn into sector 0 will be just equal to the shadow value of the forgone other output in the previous conceptual experiment.

6. Using Demand Side, Supply Side and Foreign Market Conversion Factors to Shadow Price a Good with a Variable World Price

The extension of this model to consider the case where good 0 is internationally traded, but with variable world price, is straightforward. Again we suppose that the government buys all that is supplied at a price which is incrementally above the initial consumer price, but maintains all other prices at their initial levels by meeting excess demands and supplies. In this case, the government must end up buying

$$-\bar{Q}_0 = [\eta_0 C_0 + e_0 X_0 + \sigma_0^* M_0]\hat{p}_0 \tag{9}$$

where σ_i^* is the foreign elasticity of excess supply of the ith good and M_i is the foreign excess supply of good i, i.e., home imports of it.

We define c_{d0} and c_{s0} as before, but now we also need to define the foreign trade conversion factor for the 0th commodity as the sum at shadow prices of what foreigners require in other sectors per unit value of good 0 given up. Let p_i^* be the world price of good i, M_i be home imports of i and $p_i^\dagger$ be defined as $M_i dp_i^*/dM_i + p_i^*$, holding the prices of all other tradeables constant, so this expression is simply the marginal rate of transformation of good i into foreign exchange, $\tilde{p}_i$, at constant world prices for all other goods.[1] Then, when the government raises p_0^* by purchasing good 0, and supplying unlimited quantities of all other goods at the same price as before, it must lose goods to the foreign sector with a shadow value of $-dp_0 \sum_{i \neq 0} SP_i dM_i/dp_0 = -\hat{p}_0 \sum_{i \neq 0} SP_i \sigma_{i0}^* M_i$ where σ_{i0}^* is the elasticity of foreign excess supply of the ith item with respect to the 0th world price. It must also lose foreign exchange equal to $\hat{p}_0 \{p_0^\dagger \sigma_0^* M_0 + \sum_{i \neq 0} p_i^* \sigma_{i0}^* M_i\}$, i.e., the increase in foreign exchange spent on good 0 plus that which is used up by increased foreign excess supplies of other goods. Thus, the shadow value of the package it gives up per unit value of increased imports of good zero, which we define as the foreign exchange conversion factor, can be written as

$$c_{f0} = \frac{p_0^\dagger \sigma_0^* M_0 + \sum_{i \neq 0} (p_i^* - SP_i) \sigma_{i0}^* M_i}{p_0^* \sigma_0^* M_0}. \tag{10}$$

Note that when the world price of all goods other than 0 is fixed by non-shifting foreign excess demands

$$c_{f0} = p_0^\dagger/p_0^* = \tilde{p}_0/p_0^* = 1 + \sigma_0^{*-1}. \tag{10A}$$

Finally, in the special case where the foreign sector does no saving, no foreign exchange will ever be accumulated, because the foreign sector will spend all revenues it earns from the sale of good 0 on other goods. This

---

[1] In general, the marginal rate of transformation of good 0 into foreign exchange is given by

$$\tilde{p}_0 = \sum_i M_i dp_i^*/dM_0 + p_0^*$$

where dp_i^*/dM_0 is the change in the world price of the ith good per incremental unit of good 0 supplied by the foreign sector, holding international trade in all other commodities fixed.

means that (10A) will reduce to

$$c_{f0} = - \frac{\sum\limits_{i \neq 0} SP_i \sigma^*_{i0} M_i}{p^*_0 \sigma^*_0 M_0} . \tag{10B}$$

Since domestic real income is held fixed, the shadow price of the amount of the 0th good purchased by the government is equal to the shadow price of the bundle of other goods and foreign exchange sold by the government. Thus,

$$-SP_0 \overline{Q}_0 = c_{f0} p^*_0 dM_0 - c_{d0} p^c_0 dC_0 + c_{s0} p^p_0 dX_0 . \tag{11}$$

Using

$$dM_0 = \sigma^*_0 M_0 \hat{p}^*_0 , \quad dC_0 = -\eta_0 C_0 \hat{p}^c_0 \quad \text{and} \quad dX_0 = e_0 X_0 \hat{p}^p_0 \tag{11A}$$

and equation (9), (11) can be rewritten as

$$SP_0 = \{p^c_0 \eta_0 C_0 c_{d0} + p^p_0 e_0 X_0 c_{s0} + p^*_0 \sigma^*_0 M_0 c_{f0}\}/\Delta_0 \tag{12}$$

where $\Delta_0 = \eta_0 C_0 + e_0 X_0 + \sigma^*_0 M_0 .$

Squire–van der Tak and Ray do not develop the idea of the foreign market conversion factor. Instead, they deal with foreign exchange explicitly. But that approach misses the essential symmetry which our approach highlights, and their particular analysis is valid only when the cross price elasticity of foreign excess supply of the ith good with respect to the 0th price is zero for any good i which has an imperfectly elastic foreign excess supply.

7. Shadow Pricing Policy Parameters in Terms of Other Shadow Prices

The logic of shadow pricing policy parameters is quite similar to that of shadow pricing goods as discussed in Tower (1984) and earlier in this chapter. As an example of how to use conversion factors to shadow price a policy parameter let us consider an increase in τ_0, the tariff on good 0. This results in price adjustments which mean that no official purchases of the good are undertaken. Hence:

$$0 = \bar{Q}_0 = \hat{P}_0 \left[\eta_0 C_0 + e_0 X_0 \right] + \hat{P}_0^* \sigma_0^* M_0 \qquad (13)$$

where

$$P_0 = (1 + \tau_0) P_0^* \qquad (14)$$

so

$$\hat{P}_0 = \hat{\tau}_0 + \hat{P}_0^* \qquad (15)$$

where

$$\hat{\tau}_0 = d\tau_0 / (1 + \tau_0) . \qquad (16)$$

Substituting (15) into (13) implies

$$\hat{P}_0 = \sigma_0^* M_0 \hat{\tau}_0 / \Delta_0 \qquad (17)$$

and

66

$$\hat{p}_0^* = - [\eta_0 C_0 + e_0 X_0] \hat{\tau}_0 / \Delta_0 \qquad (18)$$

where $\Delta_0 = \eta_0 C_0 + e_0 X_0 + \sigma_0^* M_0$.

Simultaneously, the government is assumed to fix real income through tax policy and to peg the prices of all other goods at their initial values by demanding or supplying them as needed along with adjusting the supply of foreign exchange. The shadow price of a policy parameter is defined as the amount of foreign exchange which the government must withdraw from the private sector in response to a unit increase in the parameter in order to leave the private sector's real income unchanged. Since real income has not changed, the shadow price of the change in the policy parameter $\hat{\tau}_0$ must be just equal to minus the shadow price of the basket of goods supplied by the government minus the foreign exchange supplied by the government. Thus the shadow price of a change in τ_0 denoted by $\hat{\tau}_0$ by is given by

$$SP\,\hat{\tau}_0 = -c_{f0} p_0^* dM_0 - c_{s0} p_0^P dX_0 + c_{d0} dC_0 \qquad (19)$$

which using (11A), (17) and (18) becomes

$$SP\,\hat{\tau}_0 = \{p_0^* [\eta_0 C_0 + e_0 X_0] c_{f0} - p_0^c \eta_0 C_0 c_{d0} - p_0^P e_0 X_0 c_{s0} \} \sigma_0^* M_0 \hat{\tau}_0 / \Delta_0 \ . \qquad (20)$$

Note that when the economy is distortionless $SP\,\hat{\tau}_0 = 0$ which is to be expected.

We leave it as an exercise for the reader to derive the analagous expressions for changes in other policy parameters like import quotas, consumption taxes, production subsidies, labor market distortions and controlled prices.

8. Shadow Pricing Autonomous Non-Policy Parameters in Terms of Other Shadow Prices

The same approach that we have been using so far in this chapter can be used to shadow price other parameters like the perceived degree of monopoly or monopsony power, technology, foreign excess supplies or world prices. Let us consider two examples.

First, suppose that there is a unit increase in the foreign excess supply of the zeroth commodity, with no change in the foreign sector's excess demands for other goods. If the government buys it up, there will be no change in domestic welfare, so the shadow price of that parameter shift is simply equal to the shadow price of the extra amount of the good supplied minus the foreign exchange that the government used to buy it.

Second, suppose that there is a 1% increase in the exogenously determined world price of good 0 with no change in foreign excess supplies of other goods. This will divert domestic production from and consumption to other goods and will cost the government foreign exchange equal to the increased foreign exchange expenditure on the 0th commodity which may be either positive or negative. Again our conceptual experiment is that the government uses taxes to keep the private sector at the same level of real income and varies excess demands and supplies of other goods to keep their prices pegged at their initial values. Thus the shadow price of a change in the world price of good 0 is given by

$$SP\hat{p_0^*} = -p_0^* dM_0 - c_{s0}p_0^P dX_0 + c_{d0}p_0^c dC_0 - M_0 dp_0^*$$

which drawing on (11A), $dM_0 + dX_0 = dC_0$ and $\hat{p_0} = \hat{p_0^P} = \hat{p_0^c} = \hat{p_0^*}$ yields

$$SP\hat{p_0^*} = \{[p_0^* - c_{s0}p_0^p]e_0X_0 + [-p_0^* + c_{d0}p_0^c]\eta_0C_0 - M_0p_0^*\}\hat{p_0^*} \cdot \qquad (21)$$

Note that if the home economy is distortionless the first two terms disappear and $SP\hat{p_0^*}$ is just minus the increased cost of good 0 which the economy was initially importing, which is to be expected.

9. Dealing with the Heterogeneity of Individual Consuming Units: An Example Involving the Shadow Pricing of a Good in Terms of the Shadow Prices of Other Goods

The basic logic of what we have already done in this chapter remains unchanged even when we no longer permit ourselves to aggregate consumer preferences as we have been doing so far. To illustrate this, we now proceed to shadow price foreign exchange in terms of the shadow prices of goods and to shadow price one good in terms of the shadow prices of others in a model with disaggregated consumer preferences.

We will define the change in social real income, dy, or real income for short, as the sum of the weighted changes in real income, dy_i, of the two price taking individuals comprising our economy, where the weights are the distribution weights (δ_i) attached by the policymaker to the individual real incomes. Thus,

$$dy = \delta_1 dy_1 + \delta_2 dy_2 \cdot \qquad (22)$$

We pretend that the government is able to vary only one shift parameter in the income tax schedule, so that it cannot redistribute income at will between the two individuals. At constant product and factor prices a fraction α_j of any tax increase is collected from the jth individual. Thus

$$dy_j = - \alpha_j dT \qquad (23)$$

where dT is the increase in taxes. Combining (22) and (23) indicates that the change in real income will be

$$dy = - dT \sum_j \alpha_j \delta_j . \qquad (24)$$

Thus the change in the quantity of the ith commodity or factor which the government will need to supply is

$$\bar{Q}_i = - [(\alpha_1 m_i^1/p_i^c) + (\alpha_2 m_i^2/p_i^c)]dT \qquad (25)$$

where m_i^j is j's marginal propensity to spend on item i out of real income. The cost to the government in foreign exchange numeraire, $\bar{F}$, of this increase in real income is the shadow price of the incremental bundle it supplies. Thus defining the real income conversion factor for the jth individual as

$$c_y^j = \sum_i m_i^j SP_i/p_i^c \qquad (26)$$

we have

$$\bar{F} = - dT \sum_j \alpha_j c_y^j . \qquad (27)$$

Combining (24) and (27) yields an expression for the shadow price of foreign exchange in real income numeraire which is given by

$$dy/\overline{F} = SPFX = (\sum_j \alpha_j \delta_j)/(\sum_j \alpha_j c_y^j) \ . \tag{28}$$

Clearly when there is only one individual in the economy, with a distribution weight of unity attached to his real income

$$dy/\overline{F} = 1/c_y^1 \tag{29}$$

which is the expression derived for the shadow price of foreign exchange in chapter II. As before, the real income conversion factor, RICF, is just the reciprocal of the shadow price of foreign exchange.

Now let's use this real income conversion factor along with the shadow prices of goods to shadow price good 0. Suppose the government releases one unit of good 0 and holds the prices of all other goods and factors constant by demanding or supplying them as necessary, but this time the government makes no attempt to hold real income constant. We can solve, using general equilibrium elasticities of demand and supply, for the change in the 0th price, dp_0. The changes in individual real incomes are given by

$$dy_j = - C_0^j dp_0^c \tag{30}$$

where C_0^j is j's initial consumption of good 0. Thus real income will have risen by

$$dy = - \sum_j \delta_j C_0^j dp_0^c \ . \tag{31}$$

At the same time the government will find itself supplying an increased amount of good i, where i > 0, given by

$$\bar{Q}_i = \sum_j (\partial c_i^j / \partial p_0^c) dp_0^c .$$

(32)

The shadow value of this bundle is given by

$$SPB = \sum_j c_{d0}^j p_0^c (dC_0^j / dp_0^c) dp_0^c$$

(33)

where c_{d0}^j is the conversion factor for expenditure diverted by the jth individual from the 0th commodity or factor and dC_0^j / dp_0^c is the change in j's consumption of the 0th commodity per unit change in p_0^c, holding all other goods and factor prices constant, but allowing real income to vary. The foreign exchange lost by the government in the process is given by

$$\bar{F} = d(M_0 p_0^*) = M_0 dp_0^* - p_0^* dM_0$$

(34)

assuming for simplicity that the foreign demand for the ith good (i > 0) is not affected by good 0's price. The shadow price of the 0th good can now be written as

$$SP_0 = RICF \cdot dy - SPB - \bar{F}$$

(35)

where dy, SPB, $\bar{F}$ and RICF are given by (31), (33), (34) and the reciprocal of (28), respectively.

10. Shadow Pricing Several Interrelated Items at Once[1]

We have presented a technique for shadow pricing a single good in terms of others. Does our approach generalize to the simultaneous shadow pricing of several items whose demands and supplies are interrelated? The answer is yes, and the generalization is straightforward. If we wish to shadow price N items which may consist of some combination of goods, factors and parameters, we need only write the N equations for each of the unknown shadow prices as in III.2 and III.3 in terms of the N-1 other unknown shadow prices and the M known shadow prices. Then we simply solve the system of N simultaneous equations for the N unknowns to simultaneously acquire all of the unknown shadow prices. If N is small, the necessary matrix inversion can be done by hand. Otherwise one would need to use a computer. However, even if N is large and one can't find a computer there is still a way out.

So far we have been working mostly with supply and demand elasticities constructed under the assumption that only one price varies. The alternative is for the shadow pricer who only knows M shadow prices to perform the following conceptual experiment. Imagine that the government withdraws one unit of good 0 from the private sector, and pegs the prices of only the M goods with known shadow prices, while letting the prices of the N goods with unknown shadow prices vary, and while compensating the private sector. The shadow price of good zero can then be calculated as the sum of the increased excess demands for the M goods with known shadow prices, each weighted by its shadow price. The only trick here is making reasonable guesses about values for these general equilibrium elasticities. Since in most cases the underlying partial equilibrium elasticities are likely to be guesses anyway,

---

[1]This section was written in response to a discussion with S. Devarajan.

such a procedure may not introduce too much additional error.

It should be noted, that this approach, which is also advocated by Sieper (1981), is another straightforward generalization of Ray's (1984) formula for shadow pricing a non-traded good or good with variable world price in terms of traded goods with fixed world prices. All we need to do is to recognize that in the presence of other non-traded goods or goods with variable world prices, the interrelation in question should be interpreted as the changes in the compensated excess demands for the traded goods (with fixed world prices) per unit change in the government's excess supply of the good in question, holding the official supplies of all other goods without fixed world prices constant.

11. The Shadow Price of Foreign Exchange when the Adjustment Mechanism Consists of Changes in Distorting Taxes

Suppose that we wish to shadow price foreign exchange, but since the mechanism by which foreign exchange is injected into or withdrawn from the economy involves changes in distorting taxes, we are unable to use the method of section II.6. Is there an alternative? Yes, and it is analogous to the method advocated there and earlier in this chapter.

If the adjustment mechanism consists of changes in selected taxes and tariffs, we can imagine that the government pegs the prices of certain goods in the face of these tax changes. Then the shadow price of foreign exchange in utility numeraire will simply be the induced change in real income defined as $dy = \sum_i p_i^c dC_i$ divided by the shadow value of the bundle of other goods which the government must supply in order to peg those prices. However, in performing these calculations, general equilibrium elasticities instead of marginal propensities to spend must be used.

We conclude that shadow pricing foreign exchange, a factor, a commodity, or a parameter in terms of other shadow prices is a conceptually very simple tool with far ranging applications.

12. A Note on the Choice of Numeraire and the Possibility of a Negative Shadow Price of Foreign Exchange

The literature on shadow pricing has settled on using either of two numeraires to shadow price. The Little-Mirrlees literature uses the amount of foreign exchange which trades for one unit of domestic currency as its numeraire; and the UNIDO (United Nations International Development Organization) literature uses a unit of domestic real income as its numeraire. However, the possible numeraires are unlimited. One could use any good, factor of production, or policy parameter as numeraire, or any bundle of goods and/or factors and/or policy parameters. In fact, in a closed economy foreign exchange is no longer a possible numeraire, and the approach most analogous to the Little-Mirrlees approach would be to use a good or factor or some bundle as numeraire.

The problem with using any arbitrary good, factor or policy parameter as numeraire is that its shadow price in real income numeraire may be negative, and if this is the case, it would be a confusing numeraire to use. The shadow price of foreign exchange in real income numeraire is likely to be positive which makes it a more suitable numeraire. However, it should be noted that Bhagwati, Brecher and Hatta (1984), Postlewaite and Webb (1984) and Yano (1984) have all discovered cases where receipt of a transfer can immiserize a country, i.e., lower its real income. That amounts to concluding that the decumulation of foreign exchange may reduce a country's real income, which is equivalent to concluding that the shadow price of foreign exchange may be negative. Their arguments hinge on more than two countries or the existence of distortions. An additional way to get a negative shadow price of foreign exchange would be to assume that the transfer was effected by an adjustment to a distorting tax in the country in question. Thus, a negative shadow price of foreign exchange is certainly a possibility.

Finally, if the transfer is effected by non-distorting taxes and subsidies in the domestic economy, the shadow price of foreign exchange will continue to be equal to the reciprocal of the sum of the values of the domestic marginal propensities to spend evaluated at shadow prices, so the shadow price of foreign exchange in utility numeraire will necessarily be negative whenever the shadow prices of all goods with positive marginal propensities to spend on them are negative and those with negative marginal propensities are positive.

Chapter IV

SHADOW PRICING IN AN ECONOMY WITH NO INTERRELATIONS BETWEEN THE

DEMANDS FOR NON TRADED GOODS AND TRADED GOODS WITH

VARIABLE WORLD PRICES, AND A FIXED EQUILIBRIUM WAGE RATE

1. Introduction

It is well known from Little-Mirrlees (1974) that the shadow prices of

goods which are tradeable at fixed world prices (with foreign exchange as the

numeriare) are simply their world prices, i.e. the amount of foreign exchange

that they trade for.[1] However, shadow pricing goods with foreign excess

demands or supplies that are not perfectly elastic and non-traded goods or

non-traded factors of production is more complex. In this chapter we present

formulae for shadow pricing goods with imperfectly elastic foreign excess

demands, labor services and foreign exchange. Moreover, we tie this in

explicitly with the inter-industry nature of production, so in our resulting

expressions the implicit rate of value added subsidy plays an important role.

The procedure for deriving shadow prices of goods and non-traded goods in

a full fledged general equilibrium model with many distortions is laid out in

Tower (1984, Chapter II). However, to deal with all of the interrelations

considered there for an economy of more than two sectors, one would need to

calculate shadow prices by computer. In this chapter, we have made some

---

[1]This holds only so long as they are not subject to quantitative import or
export restrictions so that the fixity of world prices fixes their domestic
prices. When goods are subject to binding quantitative import or export
restrictions they are treated as non-traded goods since on the margin they are
non-traded. On this see Bhagwati and Srinivasan (1981).

assumptions in order to drastically simplify the expressions for the shadow prices.These assumptions follow.

There are three types of goods, traded goods subject to variable world prices, traded goods with fixed world prices and non-traded goods. All goods are produced with a constant returns to scale (CRS) production function which uses intermediate goods and a value added aggregate in fixed proportions, and the value added aggregate is a CRS aggregate of labor which is perfectly mobile between industries and a sector specific factor of production which can be some combination of land, other natural resources, buildings and machines, but for simplicity we refer to as capital. Moreover labor and capital can be used in variable proportions.[1]

There are import and export tariffs and/or subsidies, no quotas, perfect competition and no externalities. Finally we permit excise taxes on domestic consumption, and differentials in the wages paid by various industries. Any one of four stories may be used to explain why these differentials exist: unions which bargain successfully for wage differentials, differential taxes on value added, differential payroll taxes, or minimum wages expressed as differentials between the wage paid in the ith industry and a standard wage rate. Also, some industries are covered by minimum wages which are frozen in units of foreign currency. Three restrictions give us enormous help in keeping the analysis tractable. One is that except where noted no nontraded goods or tradeable goods with variable world prices are used as intermediate inputs domestically. The second is that, holding real income constant, the domestic demand for each tradeable, non-tradeable or traded good with variable world price depends solely on its price relative to a basket of goods which is

---

[1] Alternatively, as mentioned in chapter II, we may think of capital as an intermediate input and treat the sector specific factor as labor with sector specific skills and/or training and/or sector specific venture finance.

traded at fixed world prices. The third assumption is that there is only one good which is both traded at fixed world prices and whose value added is produced with labor alone, which assures that the good in question is in perfectly elastic supply so that when additional labor is required by other sectors it is necessarily withdrawn from this sector.

Conceptually we imagine a fixed exchange rate and a flexible standard domestic wage which maintains full employment, although the analysis applies equally well to an economy with an inflexible standard wage and a flexible exchange rate, with the results being precisely the same.

2. Deriving the Fundamental Equation of Shadow Pricing

In order to derive shadow prices we start with a variant of equation (16) of section V.2 of Tower (1984), which in that paper is called the fundamental equation. It is derived and explained intuitively in Tower (1984), so we will only briefly derive it and define terms here. The one difference between this derivation and the previous one is that in this derivation we allow for only one intersectorally mobile factor, but do permit wage differentials between sectors whereas in the previous one there were many intersectorally mobile factors and no wage differentials.

Let us first define a reference price, $\tilde{p}_i$, which for exportables is simply the marginal revenue from selling abroad, $p_i^*[1 - (1/\eta_i^*)]$, with $\eta_i^* > 0$ being the elasticity of foreign excess demand, or for importables the marginal expenditure necessary to secure one unit from abroad, $p_i^*[1 + (1/\sigma_i^*)]$, where $\sigma_i^* > 0$ is the foreign elasticity of excess supply. Thus, for tradeables the reference price is the rate at which the country can transform the good in question into foreign exchange. For non-tradeables, (including goods which are subject to binding import or export quotas) $\tilde{p}_i$, is defined to be equal to the price received by producers of the good p_i^p. With these definitions we can define the consumption distortion on good i as

$$\tilde{\tau}_i = [p_i^c - \tilde{p}_i]/\tilde{p}_i \tag{1}$$

where p_i^c is the price of the ith good to consumers.

Thus if i is a non-tradeable, $\tilde{\tau}_i$ is simply the excise tax on its consumption, while if i is traded at fixed world prices, $\tilde{\tau}_i$ is simply the import tariff or export subsidy for it is the proportion by which price to consumers exceeds world price.

Unit disposable value added (where unit value added means value added per unit of output) is v_i^d. It is equal to gross unit value added v_i^g reduced by the value added tax, VAT_i:

$$v_i^d = v_i^g(1 - VAT_i). \tag{2}$$

We define reference unit value added as unit value added at reference prices:

$$\tilde{v}_i = \tilde{p}_i - \sum_j a_{ji}\tilde{p}_j \tag{3}$$

where a_{ij} is a physical input/output coefficient.

This enables us to define the value added distortion as

$$\tilde{z}_i = [v_i^d - \tilde{v}_i]/\tilde{v}_i. \tag{4}$$

When there are no non-tradeables we define the effective rate of protection as

$$ERP_i = (v_i^g - v_i^*)/v_i^* \tag{5}$$

where v_i^* is unit value added at world prices.

Thus when world prices are fixed and there are no tariffs $\tilde{z}_i$ is the explicit value added subsidy on good i, while if world prices are fixed and there is no explicit value added tax or subsidy $\tilde{z}_i$ is simply ERP_i, the effective rate of protection of the ith sector.

Therefore, $\tilde{\tau}_i$ is the proportion by which the price of a good to consumers exceeds its marginal rate of transformation into foreign exchange or else its price to producers while $\tilde{z}_i$ is the proportion by which the price of the commodity basket produced by the ith sector (which contains inputs in negative quantities) to producers in that sector exceeds its marginal rate of transformation into foreign exchange or else its price to domestic producers of the various goods in the basket.

Since consumers are supposed to spend all income, the change in their real income is given by the changes in their consumption, weighted by the prices they face:

$$dy = \sum_i p_i^c dC_i. \tag{6}[1]$$

We define the exchange rate as unity,[2] and the increase in the rate at

---

[1]Actually we do not need to assume that consumers spend all their income. If savings is permitted we can redefine dy as the change in real expenditure and the analysis of the paper is unchanged.

[2]This is the standard Little-Mirrlees (1974) device of defining a unit of foreign exchange as a "border rupee," i.e. the amount that sells for a unit of domestic currency.

which foreign exchange reserves are used up is given by

$$\bar{F} = \sum_i \tilde{p}_i dM_i \tag{7}$$

where M_i is net imports of the ith good. Thus if the ith good is exported M_i is negative.

The change in the total net product of the economy, valued at reference prices can be written either as the value of increased net output of each good summed over all goods, $\sum_i \tilde{p}_i dQ_i$, or else as the value of a unit basket of goods produced in each sector multiplied by the change in the number of baskets produced by that sector, $\sum_i \tilde{v}_i dX_i$. Thus

$$\sum_i \tilde{p}_i dQ_i = \sum_i \tilde{v}_i dX_i \tag{8}$$

where Q_i is net output of good i, i.e. gross output, X_i, minus the quantity of the good used as intermediate inputs.

Let $\bar{Q}_i$ be the autonomous increase in government sales of the ith good to the private sector. Then commodity balance dictates for all i that $dM_i = dC_i - \bar{Q}_i - dQ_i$. Multiplying by $\tilde{p}_i$, summing over all commodities and substituting from (8) yields

$$\sum_i \tilde{p}_i dM_i = \sum_i \tilde{p}_i [dC_i - \bar{Q}_i] - \sum_i \tilde{v}_i dX_i. \tag{9}$$

We pretend that the economy is competitive and there is only one mobile factor of production, so

$$v_i^d dX_i = w_i dL_i \tag{10}$$

where

$$w_i = w(1 + b_i) \qquad (11)$$

b_i is the proportion by which the wage in the ith sector, w_i, exceeds the reference wage w and L_i is employment of labor, the only mobile factor, in the ith sector.

Since there is full employment

$$\sum_i dL_i = \bar{L} \qquad (12)$$

where $\bar{L}$ is the autonomous reduction in government purchases of labor services. Combining (10), (11) and (12) yields

$$\sum_i \frac{v_i^d dX_i}{1 + b_i} = w\bar{L}. \qquad (13)$$

Combining (6), (7), (9) and (13) yields

$$dy - \bar{F} = \sum_i [p_i^c - \tilde{p}_i]dC_i - \sum_i [\frac{v_i^d}{1+b_i} - \tilde{v}_i]dX_i + \sum_i \tilde{p}_i\bar{Q}_i + w\bar{L}. \qquad (14)$$

Defining

$$\tilde{z}_{bi} = [\frac{v_i^d}{1+b_i} - \tilde{v}_i]/\tilde{v}_i \qquad (15)$$

and substituting from (1) and (15) into (14) yields

$$dy - \bar{F} = \sum_i \tilde{\tau}_i\tilde{p}_i dC_i - \sum_i \tilde{z}_{bi}\tilde{v}_i dX_i + \sum_i \tilde{p}_i\bar{Q}_i + w\bar{L}. \qquad (16)$$

If we pretend all goods are traded at fixed world prices and assume away wage differentials and taxes except tariffs, $\tilde{\tau}_i$ becomes the ith import tariff or export subsidy and $\tilde{z}_{bi}$ becomes the ith ERP. Then if we suppress the terms in $\bar{F}$, $\bar{Q}$ and $\bar{L}$, (16) becomes Bertrand's (1972) equation (15).

Now let us define

$$\tilde{\tau}_i^* = \tilde{\tau}_i / (1 + \tilde{\tau}_i) \qquad (17)$$

and

$$\tilde{z}_{bi}^* = \tilde{z}_{bi} / (1 + \tilde{z}_{bi}) \qquad (18)$$

so that $\tilde{\tau}_i^*$ is the consumption distortion on the ith good expressed as a proportion of consumers' price and $\tilde{z}_{bi}^*$ is the value-added-cum-factor-market distortion expressed as a fraction of value added at prices to producers in the ith sector. Now (1), (15), (17) and (18) can be used to rewrite (16) as

$$dy - \bar{F} = \sum_i \tilde{\tau}_i^* \, p_i^c dC_i - \sum_i \tilde{z}_{bi}^* \, \frac{v_i^d}{1+b_i} \, dX_i + \sum_i \tilde{p}_i \bar{Q}_i + w\bar{L} \qquad (19)$$

which using (10) and (11) can be expressed as

$$dy - \bar{F} = \sum_i \tilde{\tau}_i^* \, p_i^c dC_i - \sum_i \tilde{z}_{bi}^* wdL_i + \sum_i \tilde{p}_i \bar{Q}_i + w\bar{L}. \qquad (20)$$

Equation (20) is our fundamental equation of shadow pricing and is used throughout the monograph. We interpret it as follows. We assume that the government uses some behind the scenes tax and subsidy policy to hold real income (y) constant. Then holding real income constant, the amount of foreign exchange which the government is able to save $(-\bar{F})$ increases whenever consumption is shifted from sectors with low consumption distortions to sectors with high consumption distortions by the value of the consumption shift measured at consumer prices times the difference in the distortions in the two sectors.

Similarly foreign exchange savings rise by the value of labor shifted out of

high production-cum-labor-market-distortion sectors into low distortion

sectors by an amount equal to the value of labor shifted at reference wage

multiplied by the distortion differential. Thus foreign exchange is saved

whenever consumption is diverted toward more highly protected sectors and

labor is diverted from more highly protected sectors. Also, an autonomous

increase in the private sector's endowment of any good (or labor) causes

foreign exchange savings to rise by the endowment increase multiplied by the

good's reference price (or the wage rate) if we hold consumption and resource

allocation in distorted sectors constant. Clearly the right hand side of (20)

measures $-\bar{F}$ which is the foreign exchange saved by the authorities due to a

project which causes $\bar{Q}_i$s, $\bar{L}$, Ls and Cs to change combined with a tax cum

subsidy policy which fixes y. Thus we can use this equation to calculate the

shadow price of anything a la Little-Mirrlees as the extra foreign exchange

which would be necessary for the government to give up to compensate the

private sector for loss of one unit of the item.[1] Finally, as mentioned

above, for more on the logic of equation (20) see Tower (1984, Ch. V).

As a postscript, it should be noted that there are a number of useful

forms that the fundamental equation of shadow pricing can take. For example,

----

[1]This is the same interpretation of shadow prices as used by Sieper (1980).
It is necessary to specify what we mean by compensation here. The easiest
assumption is to postulate that all members of the private sector have identical tastes and factor ownership, so that any economic change will effect all
equally. Alternatively we can assume that the government is able to
redistribute income costlessly and does so in such a way that it maximizes a
Bergsonian welfare function. Then the government instead of adjusting taxes
to keep everyone as well off as initially, makes adjustments which keep the
economy on the same social indifference curve, and the compensated demand
elasticities will be calculated with reference to the given social indifference curve. On ways to rationalize social indifference curves see Tower
(1979).

we can combine (6), (7), and (9), while supressing the $\overline{Q}_i$ and assuming that the government adjusts income taxes to keep real income, y, fixed in order to yield

$$-\overline{F} = \sum (p_i^c - \tilde{p}_i)dC_i + \sum \tilde{v}_i dX_i$$

where $-\overline{F}$ is the foreign exchange saved by the government. This implies, as noted in chapter I, that we can express the shadow price of a factor of production as the sum of the induced changes in net outputs valued at reference prices plus the sum of changed consumption valued at differences between consumer prices and reference prices, where these induced changes follow from release of a unit of the factor services by the government and the government has compensated the private sector, by varying income taxes. Here our net outputs have been expressed as baskets of goods produced by each sector as discussed in section (II.6), with the reference price being the reference price of value added, but just as in (II.6) we could equally well have disaggregated the value added basket into inputs and outputs and evaluated each at their reference prices.[1]

---

[1]Our fundamental equation of shadow pricing has a number of antecedents in the literature, besides Bertrand (1972). Smith's (1982) equation (25) is virtually identical except that it does not allow for the interindustry structure of production, it assumes that all goods are traded and it allows for shifts in foreign excess demands. Also, see Sieper (1981), p. 26. An early antecedent of this whole literature is Bhagwati, Ramaswami and Srinivasan (1969).

3. Deriving Shadow Prices of Goods and Labor

We break the N goods which are consumed domestically down into N_h goods which are not traded at fixed world prices, which for short we will call home goods and N_t goods which are traded at fixed world prices and we will call traded goods. The class of home goods consists of non-traded goods and traded goods with upward sloping foreign excess supply curves or downward sloping foreign excess demand curves.

To make the analysis tractable we need to impose certain restrictions on demand. The restriction that we select is that consumption of the ith traded good depends only on the price of the ith home good given that real income and the consumer price of the ith traded good are both held constant. Moreover, the consumption of the ith home good depends only on its price, also holding real income and traded goods prices constant.[1] Denote the price of the ith home good to consumers, producers and the world by h_i^c, h_i^p and h_i^* respectively, where if the good is not traded at all h_i^* is undefined, and denote consumption of the ith home good by H_i. Denote the corresponding variables for the ith traded good by π_i^c, π_i^p, π_i^* and Π_i. Equation (6) combined with our restriction on demand implies that for a given level of real income it must be true that

$$h_i^c dH_i + \pi_i^c d\Pi_i = 0. \tag{21}$$

Thus any reduction in consumption of the one good must be matched by an increase of equal value in consumption of the other good.

---

[1]This amounts to postulating a utility function with no substitutability between composite commodities, where the ith composite commodity is a variable proportions combination of the ith home and the ith tradeable good.

When specifying consumption demand for the ith tradeable good we define that good as the composite of traded goods which substitutes in consumption for the ith home good. Thus, while we will refer to it as a single good with a single tariff, the reader can imagine that we are dealing with a composite good. This means that the tariff on the ith tradeable which is used in the analysis of consumption refers to a weighted average of the tariffs on the relevant tradeables where the weights are calculated from the proportions of expenditure that are diverted to the various tradeables when the price of the ith home good rises.

While this assumption about the structure of demand seems very stringent it is implicit in Ray (1984, Chapter 4) and also in much of the analysis of Squire and van der Tak (1975), especially pp. 144 and 145.

For tractability sake we also need to impose restrictions on the supply side. We choose to pretend that value added in sector 0 is produced using labor alone and that the world price of good 0 and all of its inputs are fixed. This means that sector 0 will have a perfectly elastic demand for labor. We pretend that this is true in no other sector, which means that if labor demand in some other sector increases, labor will be drawn from sector 0 to fill that demand. Thus we find it useful to write our full employment condition as

$$dL_o + \sum_{i \neq o} dL_i = \bar{L}. \tag{22}$$

Substituting (21) and (22) into (20) while holding y constant yields

$$-\bar{F} = \sum_i [\tilde{\tau}^*_{hi} - \tilde{\tau}^*_{\pi i}]h^c_i dH_i - \sum_{i \neq 0} [\tilde{z}^*_{bi} - \tilde{z}^*_{b0}]wdL_i + \sum \tilde{p}_i \bar{Q}_i + w[1 - \tilde{z}^*_{b0}]\bar{L}. \tag{23}$$

Since we are holding y constant

$$\hat{H}_i = -\eta_i \hat{h}_i^c \tag{24}$$

where a hat, "^," denotes a proportional change and $\eta_i > 0$ is the compensated elasticity of demand for the ith home good.

Domestic supply of each good is

$$\hat{X}_i = \varepsilon_i \hat{p}_i^p \tag{25}$$

where $\varepsilon_i > 0$ is the elasticity of supply of good i.[1]

Net exports, E, of each good are given by

$$\hat{E}_i = -\eta_i^* \hat{p}_i^* \tag{26}$$

where $\eta_i^* > 0$ is the foreign elasticity of excess demand for i and net exports are exports minus imports.

Since by definition there are no quantitative restrictions on traded goods and because all taxes and tariffs are ad valorem, $\hat{p}_i^c = \hat{p}_i^p$ and $\hat{h}_i^c = \hat{h}_i^p$. Moreover, when $\hat{p}_i^*$ and $\hat{h}_i^*$ are defined it is true that

$$\hat{p}_i^c = \hat{p}_i^p = \hat{p}_i^* \quad \text{and} \quad \hat{h}_i^c = \hat{h}_i^p = \hat{h}_i^* . \tag{27}$$

This enables us to write proportional price changes without superscripts when

---

[1]From equation (6') of chapter II of Tower (1984) $\varepsilon_i = \sigma_i v_{Li}/[(1-v_{Li})\theta_{vi}]$ where σ_i is the elasticity of substitution between labor and the fixed factor in producing value added, v_{Li} is the share of labor in disposable value added and θ_{vi} is the share of gross value added in output. It is also shown there that $\varepsilon_i = e_i/\theta_{vi}$ where e is the elasticity of supply with respect to the wage rate or as we discussed in the previous chapter with respect to the price of value added.

it suits us.

Commodity balance dictates

$$dH_i + dE_i = \bar{Q}_i + dX_i \qquad (28)$$

Combining (24) – (28) implies

$$\hat{h}_i^c = -\bar{Q}_i/D_i \qquad (29)$$

where

$$D_i = H_i \eta_i + X_i \varepsilon_i + E_i \eta_i^* , \qquad (30)$$

and these variables refer to the ith home good.

From equation (6) of chapter II of Tower (1983)

$$\hat{X}_i = v_{Li} \hat{L}_i \qquad (31)$$

where v_{Li} is the share of labor in disposable value added in the production of i.

Recognizing that disposable value added in sector i, V_i is given by

$$V_i = w_i L_i / v_{Li} \qquad (32)$$

we can combine (25), (27), (31) and (32) to yield

$$w_i dL_i = \varepsilon_i V_i \hat{p}_i^c. \qquad (33)$$

Substituting this and (29) combined with (24) into (23) while remembering

89

(11) and that the reference price of the ith tradeable is π_i^* yields

$$-\bar{F} = \sum_i \pi_i^* \bar{\Pi}_i + w[1 - \tilde{z}_{b0}^*]\bar{L}$$

(34)

$$+ \sum_i [\tilde{h}_i + \frac{(\tilde{\tau}_{hi}^* - \tilde{\tau}_{\pi i}^*)h_i^c \eta_i H_i + (\tilde{z}_{bi}^* - \tilde{z}_{b0}^*)\varepsilon_i V_i/(1 + b_i)}{D_i}]\bar{H}_i$$

where $\bar{\Pi}$ and $\bar{H}$ are the changes in the private sector's endowments of the ith
tradeable and ith home good respectively, and D_i refers to the ith home good.

4. Calculating Shadow Prices of Goods and Labor

Equation (34) gives us the information that we need to calculate shadow
prices. The coefficient of any variable with a bar over it gives us the
amount of foreign exchange which can be saved when one unit of the good in
question or factor is released by the government to the private sector, and
still leave the private sector as well off as before. This then is its shadow
price.

Reassuringly, the shadow prices of goods which are traded at fixed world
prices are given by those world prices. The reason for this is clear. If the
private sector is endowed with an extra unit of a traded good it will attempt
to trade it initially for foreign exchange which will then be used to purchase
a variety of goods. Before the private sector can spend it, the government is
assumed to tax this foreign exchange away from them, leaving the private
sector in precisely the same equilibrium as before but with governmental
reserves of foreign exchange augmented by the foreign exchange which the good
in question fetched on the world market.

The shadow price of labor is simply $w[1 - \tilde{z}^*_{b0}]$. Good 0 is tradeable and uses only tradeable goods as intermediate inputs. Moreover, we define its wage as the reference wage so by definition it has no labor market distortion. This means that we can use (2), (4), (5) and (18) to obtain

$$\tilde{z}^*_{bo} = \frac{z_0}{1 + z_0} \tag{35}$$

where

$$z_o = \tilde{z}_o = (1 - VAT_0)(1 + ERP_0) - 1 \tag{36}$$

and z_i is defined in Tower (1984) chapter IV as the effective rate of value added subsidy.

This calculation makes good sense. The shadow price of labor is simply the amount of foreign exchange that one more unit of labor would earn, and that is its wage reduced by the implicit subsidy to its use in sector 0, which is the sector to which it would be allocated if additional labor supplies become available. The reason that the formula for the shadow price of labor is such a simple one is that additional units of labor are employed in producing one good whose price is fixed, so that until labor's earnings are spent no prices change, and then before those earnings can be spent the government taxes them away. This leaves the private sector exactly as before, but with the government richer by the amount of foreign exchange that the additional labor has earned.

The complex expressions are the coefficients of the various $\bar{H}_i$. These coefficients indicate that the shadow price of each of those goods is equal to its reference price with certain adjustments. Release of an additional quantity of the ith home good to the private sector will lower its price and divert consumption from competing tradeables into the good in question, thereby saving foreign exchange. But the foreign exchange saved will be less, the more that consumption of this tradeable is implicitly taxed relative to the home good. Similarly making more of the ith home good available to the private sector will lower domestic production of the good and to the extent that production of this good is implicitly subsidized to a lesser extent than the activity into which factors are squeezed there is a further reduction in foreign exchange saved. The demand effect will be more important relative to the supply effect the larger is the demand elasticity relative to the supply elasticity. In the limiting case of an infinite foreign elasticity of excess demand D_i approaches infinity and the shadow price of H_i is given by its reference price, which is the world price and is to be expected. Finally, in the special case when the domestic demand elasticity is large, i.e. where $\eta_i \gg \varepsilon_i$, η_i^* the shadow price of the ith home good is

$$SPHI = \tilde{h}_i + \left[\tilde{\tau}_{hi}^* - \tilde{\tau}_{\pi i}^*\right]h_i^c \qquad (37)$$

and when the supply elasticity is large, i.e. $\varepsilon_i \gg \eta_i$, η_i^*, the shadow price of the ith home good is

$$SPHI = \tilde{h}_i + (\tilde{z}_{bi}^* - \tilde{z}_{b0}^*)V_i/[X_i(1 + b_i)] = \tilde{h}_i + (\tilde{z}_{bi}^* - \tilde{z}_{b0}^*)h_i^p\theta_{vi}^d/(1 + b_i) \qquad (38)$$

where θ_{vi}^d is the share of disposable value added in output of the ith home good.

There is no conflict between this formula and those in Ray (1984) or the formula for shadow pricing non-traded goods in Squire and van der Tak (1975, p. 145). One apparent difference is not substantive: the other authors simply choose to combine the elements making up the coefficient of $\bar{H}_i$ differently. In particular, they divide $\tilde{h}_i$ by D_i. We have broken $\tilde{h}_i$ out because conceptually it seems easiest to think of a shadow price as being a reference price to which adjustments are added per our expressions.

We have tried to provide several services here. First we have stressed the nature of the conceptual model that gives rise to these results. Second, we have come to the conclusion that what is relevant for the shadow price formulae is the compensated demand elasticity whereas the other authors were not specific on this. Third we have dealt for the first time (except for Pursell (1978)) with the problem of the input-output structure, and thereby have shown how the concept of effective protection relates to the problem.[1] Fourth, we have shown how to deal explicitly with factor market distortions, value added taxes and consumption taxes on non-traded goods. Finally, both the central project notes and Squire and van der Tak are unclear about how to calculate, α, the supply price conversion factor. As we see from (34), (37), (38) and Squire and van der Tak's (A24), in the special case where all private sector consumers are identical Squire and van der Tak's α becomes

$$\alpha_i = \tilde{h}_i + (\tilde{z}^*_{bi} - \tilde{z}^*_{bo})\theta^d_{vi} h^p_i/(1 +_i b) \tag{39}$$

and their β becomes

$$\beta_i = \tilde{h}_i + [\tilde{\tau}^*_{hi} - \tilde{\tau}^*_{\pi i}]h^c_i. \tag{40}$$

[1] Bertrand (1972; 1974) derives a special case of our fundamental equation of shadow pricing which does use the ERP, but he does not combine it with structural parameters to derive explicit expressions.

5. Coping with Monopoly, Monopsony and Intermediate Inputs with Variable
   World Prices

The formulae presented here can also be used to apply more generally than
in the circumstances considered so far. First, suppose that the producer of
some good perceives that he has monopoly power and therefore charges for his
value added some premium over cost of production. The analysis of this case
is just as before except that VAT in the formula should account for the
differential between gross and disposable value added due to the explicit
value added tax plus the monopoly mark up.

Similarly, if our producer perceives monopsony in his labor market (even
though in this model there is no monopsony power in fact) he could just aug-
ment the size of b to reflect the perceived difference between the marginal
expenditure on labor and the cost of the marginal worker as well as the actual
wage differential.

Finally, if a producer perceived that he has monopsony power in his
purchase of intermediate inputs he will charge himself an implicit tax on the
purchase of these goods which would enter the analysis just as an explicit
import tax. The only problem is that in the case of intermediate inputs whose
world prices are not fixed in order to keep the analysis simple it is
necessary to assume that the use of each such input is specific to a
particular sector and that no such good is produced or consumed at home.
Otherwise we are stuck with a messy matrix calculation.

In each of these three cases, one would also expect ε, the elasticity
of supply to be lower than it would otherwise be.

6. The Shadow Price of Foreign Exchange In Utility Numeraire

Suppose we are contemplating a project which generates a certain amount of producers' and consumers' surplus evaluated at consumers' prices which we denote by dy, as well as an amount of foreign exchange, $-\bar{F}$. If dy and $-\bar{F}$ have different signs it is necessary in some way to convert the real income change into a foreign exchange savings. In order to do this it is necessary to know how much real income it is necessary to give up in order to earn one more unit of foreign exchange. This is what Warr (1980, p. 34) refers to as "the shadow price of foreign exchange in utility <u>numeraire</u>" and what Bacha and Taylor (1971) refer to as the second best shadow price of foreign exchange. Denoting this shadow price by SPFX, we then evaluate the net benefit of the project when measured in foreign exchange as

$$\text{Net Benefit} = dy/\left[\text{SPFX}\right] + (-\bar{F}) \tag{41}$$

and the project is beneficial if and only if this expression is positive.

We could have derived SPFX by allowing y to vary in our derivation of (34) and then the coefficient of dy on the right hand side of (34) would have indicated the gain in foreign exchange of raising real income by one unit. Thus the reciprocal of this coefficient with reversed sign would be the SPFX. This procedure is, however, a bit tedious and a waste of energy since as Scott (1974) notes and we showed in section II it is just the reciprocal of the sum of the conversion factors for each of the goods, each weighted by the marginal propensity to spend on it. Note that in the special case where all goods are traded at fixed world prices $SP_i = (1-\tilde{\tau}_i^*)p_i^c$, where SP_i is the shadow price of good i, so since $\Sigma m_i = 1$, (where m_i is the marginal

95

propensity to spend on i), reflecting that all income is spent

$$\text{SPFX} = \frac{1}{\sum\limits_i (1-\tilde{\tau}_i^*)p_i^c m_i/p_i^c} = \frac{1}{\sum\limits_i (1-\tilde{\tau}_i^*)m_i} = \frac{1}{1-\sum\limits_i m_i \tilde{\tau}_i^*} \tag{42}$$

which also appears in section V.5 of Tower (1984).

Chapter V

SHADOW PRICING WHEN THE EQUILIBRIUM WAGE RATE IS VARIABLE

1. Introduction

The model of chapter IV assumed that one and only one sector had a perfectly elastic demand for labor. In this section we do away with that assumption and postulate that the demand for labor in each sector is downward sloping. The cost of this is that the analysis becomes more complex although as we shall see it is still manageable.

We use the same model as in the previous section except that we no longer postulate the elasticity of supply of good zero, ε_o, to be infinite. Also, we continue to postulate a fixed exchange rate, but now we postulate labor's wage to vary, except in those sectors where a binding minimum wage is assumed to be in force.

2. Deriving Shadow Prices

Throughout the rest of the monograph whenever we reference one chapter's equation from another chapter, we will preceed it with the chapter number. Thus chapter IV's equation (20) is referenced as (IV20) from chapter V but simply as (20) from chapter IV.

Combining (IV20), (IV21) and (IV24) with the assumption that real income is kept constant yields

$$-\bar{F} = -\sum_i \tau_i^{**} \, \eta_i p_i^c H_i \hat{h}_i - \sum_i \tilde{z}_{bi}^* w dL_i + \sum_i \tilde{p}_i \bar{Q}_i + w\bar{L} \tag{1}$$

97

where $\tilde{\tau}_i^{**} = \tilde{\tau}_{hi}^* - \tilde{\tau}_{\pi i}^*$.

We define a dummy variable μ_i which takes on a value of 1 in any sector where wages are determined competitively i.e. by market forces and 0 for sectors where minimum wages or union contracts which freeze the wage are binding. In sectors where wages are not frozen we assume that b_i is given so that $\hat{w}_i = \hat{w}$. Using this information plus equation (6') of chapter II of Tower (1984) we have

$$\hat{X} = \varepsilon_i \hat{p}_i^p - \mu_i \varepsilon_i \theta_i^v \hat{w} \tag{2}$$

which is analagous to (IV25) except that now market forces will allow wages to vary.

Combining (2), (IV24), (IV26), (IV27) and (IV28) implies

$$\hat{h}_i^c = -\alpha_i \bar{H}_i + \beta_i \hat{w} \tag{3}$$

where

$$\alpha_i = 1/D_i = 1/\left[H_i \eta_i + X_i \varepsilon_i + E_i \eta_i^*\right] \tag{4}$$

and

$$\beta_i = \mu_i \varepsilon_i \theta_i^v X_i / D_i. \tag{5}$$

Combining (2) with (IV13) yields

$$\sum_i V_i \left[\varepsilon_i \hat{p}_i - (\mu_i \varepsilon_i \theta_i^v)\hat{w}\right]/(1+b_i) = w\bar{L}. \tag{6}$$

Combining (3) and (6) yields

98

$$\hat{w} = -\gamma w\bar{L} - \sum_i \delta_i \bar{H}_i \qquad (7)$$

where

$$\gamma = 1/\sum_i \varepsilon_i V_i \beta_i^* / (1+b_i) > 0 \qquad (8)$$

$$\delta_i = \frac{\varepsilon_i V_i \alpha_i / (1+b_i)}{\sum_i \varepsilon_i V_i \beta_i^* / (1+b_i)} > 0 \qquad (9)$$

and

$$\beta_i^* = \mu_i \theta_i^v - \beta_i \geqslant 0 \ . \qquad (10)$$

Combining (3) and (7) yields

$$\hat{h}_i = -\beta_i \left[\gamma w\bar{L} + \sum_i \delta_i \bar{H}_i \right] - \alpha_i \bar{H}_i . \qquad (11)$$

Combining (IV10) and (2) yields

$$w_i dL_i = V_i \left[\varepsilon_i \hat{p}_i - \mu_i \varepsilon_i \theta_i^v \hat{w} \right]. \qquad (12)$$

Combining (7), (10), (11) and (12) yields

$$w_i dL_i = -\varepsilon_i V_i \beta_i^* \left[\gamma w\bar{L} + \sum_j \delta_j \bar{H}_j \right] - \varepsilon_i V_i \alpha_i \bar{H}_i . \qquad (13)$$

Finally combining (1), (11), (13) and (IV11) yields our equation for calculating shadow prices

$$-\bar{F} = \sum_i \pi_i^* \bar{\Pi}_i + w(1+\lambda)\bar{L}$$

$$+ \sum_i \left\{ \hat{h}_i + \frac{\lambda \varepsilon_i V_i \alpha_i}{1+b_i} + \alpha_i \left[\tilde{\tau}_i^{**} \eta_i h_i^c H_i + \frac{\tilde{z}_{bi}^* \varepsilon_i V_i}{1+b_i} \right] \right\} \bar{H}_i \qquad (14)$$

99

where

$$\lambda = \gamma\{\sum_i \tilde{\tau}_i^{**}\beta_i \eta_i h_i^C H_i + \sum_i \tilde{z}_{bi}^{*}\varepsilon_i V_i \beta_i^{*}/(1+b_i)\}. \tag{15}$$

As before the coefficients of the terms with bars over them indicate the
shadow prices of tradeables with fixed prices, $\bar{\Pi}_i$, labor $\bar{L}$ and both non-
tradeables and traded goods with variable world prices, $\bar{H}_i$. Then the shadow
price of foreign exchange in utility numeraire is simply the reciprocal of the
sum of these shadow prices each weighted by the marginal propensity to spend
on it. We leave it as an exercise for the reader to demonstrate that equations (14) and (15) collapse into (IV34) in the special case where $\varepsilon_o \to \infty$. No
new concepts emerge from (14) and (15) so no discussion is necessary.
Frequently it is probably appropriate to assume that wages will not vary so
that (IV34) will be appropriate. But (14) is presented in hopes that it will
be useful to project evaluators when a project is anticipated to influence
wages.

Chapter VI

SHADOW PRICING WHEN THE DEMAND FOR EACH GOOD DEPENDS ON ITS
PRICE RELATIVE TO A SINGLE NON-TRADED GOOD

1. Introduction

In this chapter we extend the model explored in chapter II in several
additional directions. Chapter II's analysis had to be kept simple enough to
be amenable to geometric analysis. In this chapter we shed that constraint
and therefore are forced to use mathematics similar to that of the two pre-
ceeding sections. We assume that there are three types of goods: 1. traded
goods with fixed world prices, 2. traded goods subject to variable world
prices and nontraded goods subject to diminishing returns to the variable
factor, labor, and 3. a non-traded good which we will call services. Value
added in services is assumed to be produced using labor alone. All goods are
produced with a constant returns to scale (CRS) production function which uses
intermediate goods and value added in fixed proportions, and value added is a
CRS aggregate of labor which is perfectly mobile between industries and a
sector specific factor of production which can be some combination of land,
other natural resources, buildings and machines, but for simplicity we refer
to as capital. Moreover labor and capital can be used in variable
proportions. There are import and export tariffs and/or subsidies, no quotas,
perfect competition, no externalities, and excise taxes on the domestic
consumption of all goods plus labor services. Differentials exist in the
wages paid by various industries. As before, any one of four stories may be
used to explain why these differentials exist: unions which bargain

successfully for wage differentials, differential taxes on value added,
differential payroll taxes, or minimum wages expressed as differentials
between the wage paid in the ith industry and a standard wage rate. Also,
some industries are covered by minimum wages which are frozen in units of
foreign currency. One restriction is that only traded goods with fixed world
prices are used as intermediate inputs domestically. Finally, we assume that,
holding real income constant, the domestic demand for each tradeable depends
solely on its price relative to non-traded services. This is the difference
between the model developed here and that in chapter V.

2. The Model

Our goal is to shadow price goods and labor with foreign exchange as the
numeraire. Then as discussed in chapter II it is an easy matter to obtain the
shadow price of foreign exchange in utility numeraire.

Our strategy is to develop the various equations which describe how
wages, prices, goods flows and factor flows depend on autonomous official
transfers (gifts or sales) of labor and goods to the private sector. Then we
plug these into the fundamental equation of shadow pricing to obtain our
shadow prices. We have from (V2) the domestic supply function for each good:

$$\hat{X}_i = \varepsilon_i \hat{p}_i^p - (\mu_i \varepsilon_i \theta_i^v)\hat{w} \tag{1}$$

where X_i is domestic output, ε_i is the elasticity of supply, p^p is the price
of i to producers, and θ_i^v is the share of gross value added in output. μ_i is a
dummy variable which takes on a value of unity if the wage is sector i is
either market determined or differs from the standard wage by a constant

proportion b_i, and it takes on a value of zero if the wage in sector i is fixed by a wage contract or a legal minimum. From (IV26) net exports of i, E_i, are given by

$$\hat{E}_i = -\eta_i^* \hat{p}_i^* \tag{2}$$

where $\eta_i^* > 0$ is the compensated elasticity of foreign excess demand and p_i^* is world price.

From (IV28) material balance dictates

$$dC_i + dE_i = \bar{Q}_i + dQ_i \tag{3}$$

where $\bar{Q}_i$ is the autonomous increase in government sales of good i to the private sector, and Q_i is the economy's net output of good i. We assume that the exchange rate is permanently fixed at unity and that all taxes, tariffs and subsidies are ad valorem. Thus $\hat{p}_i^p = \hat{p}_i^c$ and assuming that the good is traded so that $\hat{p}_i^*$ is defined, the proportional changes in the producers', consumers' and world price are all identical, so that in writing proportional changes in prices we can dispense with superscripts and write

$$\hat{p}_i^c = \hat{p}_i^p = \hat{p}_i^* = \hat{p}_i. \tag{4}$$

Services we label as good 0, and since value added in services is produced with labor alone $\varepsilon_0 \to \infty$. Thus from (1) and (4), $\hat{p}_0^p = \mu_i \theta_i^v \hat{w}$. Since we assume that holding real income, y, constant, the demand for the ith good depends on its price relative to services we have for $i > 0$

$$\hat{C}_i = -\eta_i \left[\hat{p}_i - \mu_0 \theta_0^v \hat{w} \right] \tag{5}$$

where C_i is consumption of good i and η_i is the compensated elasticity of demand for it. We pretend that no good without a fixed world price is used as an intermediate input. Thus for non-traded goods and goods with variable world prices $Q_i = X_i$ which means for them (1) – (5) can be combined to yield

$$\hat{p}_i = \omega_i \hat{w} - \alpha_i \bar{Q}_i \tag{6}$$

where

$$\omega_i = \left[\eta_i C_i \mu_0 \theta_0^v + (\mu_i \varepsilon_i \theta_i^v) X_i \right] / \left[\eta_i C_i + \varepsilon_i X_i + \eta_i^* E_i \right] \tag{7}$$

and

$$\alpha_i = 1 / \left[\eta_i C_i + \varepsilon_i X_i + \eta_i^* E_i \right]. \tag{8}$$

We have defined (6) to hold only when $\eta_i^* < \infty$. But when $\eta_i^* \to \infty$, we know from the law of one price that $\hat{p}_i = 0$ so that both ω_i and α_i in (6) must equal zero. Equations (7) and (8) satisfy this constraint. Therefore, (6), (7) and (8) apply even for commodities with fixed prices.

Equations (1) and (6) enable us to write

$$\hat{X}_i = -(\varepsilon_i^* \theta_i^v) \hat{w} - \alpha_i \varepsilon_i \bar{Q}_i \tag{9}$$

where

$$\varepsilon_i^* = \varepsilon_i \left[\mu_i - (\omega/\theta_i^v) \right]. \tag{10}$$

Equations (5) and (6) combine to yield

$$dC_i = \bar{\eta}_i C_i \hat{w} + \eta_i C_i \alpha_i \bar{Q}_i \tag{11}$$

where

$$\bar{\eta}_i = \eta_i(\mu_0\theta_0^v - \omega_i). \tag{12}$$

Combining (IV10), (IV11) and $V_i = X_i v_i^d$ where V_i and v_i^d are respectively total and unit disposable value added in sector i yields

$$wdL_i = \frac{v_i^d dX_i}{1+b_i} = \frac{V_i\hat{X}_i}{1+b_i} \tag{13}$$

where b_i is the proportion by which the wage in sector i exceeds the standard wage, and L_i is employment in the ith sector.

Combining (9) and (13) yields

$$wdL_i = -\frac{V_i}{1+b_i}\left[(\varepsilon_i^*\theta_i^v)\hat{w} + \alpha_i\varepsilon_i\bar{Q}_i\right]. \tag{14}$$

Full employment dictates

$$dL_0 + \sum_{i\neq 0} dL_i = \bar{L} \tag{15}$$

where $\bar{L}$ is the autonomous release of labor by the government to the private sector. Our shadow prices are measured in quantities of foreign exchange holding real income, y, constant. The definition of real income combined with this constancy implies

$$dy = \sum_{i\neq 0} p_i^c dC_i + p_0^c dC_0 = 0. \tag{16}$$

Equations (11) and (16) combine to yield

$$p_0^c dC_0 = -\sum_{i\neq 0}(\bar{\eta}_i p_i^c C_i \hat{w} + \eta_i p_i^c C_i \alpha_i \bar{Q}_i). \tag{17}$$

Since labor is the only input into value added in the zeroth sector

$$\frac{(1+b_0)w\ dL_o}{p_0^c dX_0} = \frac{w_0 L_0}{p_0^c X_0}.$$ (18)

Thus we can write

$$wdL_0 = \theta_0^L p_0^c dX_0$$ (19)

where

$$\theta_o^L = \frac{w_0 L_0}{(1+b_0)p_0^c X_o}$$ (20)

and θ_0^L is the share of labor at reference wage in output evaluated at consumer prices in the zeroth sector.

Combining (17) and (19) while recognizing that $dC_o = dX_o$ yields

$$wdL_o = -\theta_o^L \sum_{i \neq 0} (\bar{\eta}_i p_i^c C_i \hat{w} + \eta_i p_i^c C_i \alpha_i \bar{Q}_i).$$ (21)

Equations (14), (15) and (21) combine to yield

$$\hat{w} = -\beta_L \bar{L} - \sum_{i \neq 0} \beta_i \bar{Q}_i$$ (22)

where

$$\beta_L = w/\delta$$ (23)

$$\beta_i = [\theta_0^L \eta_i p_i^c C_i + \frac{\varepsilon_i V_i}{1+b_i}]\alpha_i/\delta$$ (24)

and

$$\delta = \sum_{i \neq 0} (\theta_0^L \bar{\eta}_i p_i^c C_i + \frac{\varepsilon_i^* V_i \theta_i^V}{1+b_i}).$$ (25)

From (IV23) we know that the fundamental equation of shadow pricing is

$$-\bar{F} = \sum \tilde{\tau}_i^{**} p_i^c dC_i - \sum_i (\tilde{z}_{bi}^* - \tilde{z}_{b0}^*) w dL_i + \sum \tilde{p}_i \bar{Q}_i + w\bar{L} \qquad (26)$$

where

$$\tilde{\tau}_i^{**} = \tilde{\tau}_i^* - \tilde{\tau}_0^* \qquad (27)$$

and $\tilde{\tau}_i^*$ is the consumption distortion in the ith sector expressed as a fraction of the price to consumers. In the particular model we are constructing in this section assuming good i is traded, $\tilde{p}_i = (1 - \frac{1}{\eta^*}) p_i^*$ and $p_i^c = (1+t_i)(1+e_i) p_i^*$ where t_i is the import tariff or export subsidy expressed as a proportion of the world price and e_i is the excise tax on domestic consumption of good i expressed as a proportion of its domestic price. Thus for a traded good

$$\tilde{\tau}_i^* = \frac{p_i^c - \tilde{p}_i}{p_i^c} = \frac{(1+t_i)(1+e_i)(1- \frac{1}{\eta_i^*})^{-1} - 1}{(1+t_i)(1+e_i)(1- \frac{1}{\eta_i^*})^{-1}} \qquad (28)$$

and for a nontraded good $p_i^c = (1+t_i)(1+e_i)\tilde{p}_i$ so

$$\tilde{\tau}_i^* = \frac{(1+t_i)(1+e_i) - 1}{(1+t_i)(1+e_i)} \qquad (29)$$

which means that (28) continues to describe the distortion with η_i^* set equal to infinity.

For services

$$\tilde{\tau}_0^* = \frac{e_0}{1+e_0}. \qquad (30)$$

Thus

$$\tilde{\tau}_i^{**} = \frac{1}{1+e_0} \left[\frac{(1+t_i)(1+e_i)(1-\frac{1}{\eta_i^*})^{-1} - (1+e_0)}{(1+t_i)(1+e_0)(1-\frac{1}{\eta_i^*})^{-1}} \right]. \tag{31}$$

Substituting (22) into (11) and (14) and the result into (26) yields

$$-\bar{F} = \sum_{i \neq 0} \tilde{\tau}_i^{**} \{ \bar{\eta}_i p_i^c C_i [-\beta_L \bar{L} - \sum_{j \neq 0} \beta_j \bar{Q}_j] + \eta_i p_i^c C_i \alpha_i \bar{Q}_i \}$$

$$- \sum_{i \neq 0} (\tilde{z}_{bi}^* - \tilde{z}_{b0}^*) \{ \frac{V_i}{1+b_i} (\varepsilon_i^* \theta_i^V)(\beta_L \bar{L} + \sum_{j \neq 0} \beta_j \bar{Q}_j) - \alpha_i \varepsilon_i \bar{Q}_i \} + w\bar{L} + \sum_i \tilde{p}_i \bar{Q}_i \tag{32}$$

which can be rearranged to yield

$$-\bar{F} = (1-k)w\bar{L}$$

$$+ \sum_{i \neq 0} \{ \tilde{p}_i + \alpha_i [\sum_{j \neq 0} k_j (\frac{\varepsilon_i V_i}{1+b_i} + \theta_0^L \eta_i p_i^c C_i) + \tilde{\tau}_i^{**} \eta_i p_i^c C_i + (\tilde{z}_{bi}^* - \tilde{z}_{b0}^*) \frac{\varepsilon_i V_i}{1+b_i}] \} \bar{Q}_i \tag{33}$$

where

$$k = \frac{\sum \tilde{\tau}_i^{**} \bar{\eta}_i p_i^c C_i + (\tilde{z}_{bi}^* - \tilde{z}_0^*) \frac{V_i \varepsilon_i^* \theta_i^V}{1+b_i}}{\sum_{i \neq 0} (\theta_0^L \bar{\eta}_i p_i^c C_i + \frac{\varepsilon_i^* V_i \theta_i^V}{1+b_i})}. \tag{34}$$

As before the coefficients of $\bar{L}$ and $\bar{Q}_i$ are the shadow prices of labor and goods in the model. We have achieved our goal. If there are no distortions the shadow price of labor is w and of goods is $\tilde{p}_i$ which in this special case is $p_i = p_i^p = p_i^c$.

Equation (33) is somewhat intractable. However, in the special case where all world prices are fixed, all goods are traded except services,

108

services are produced using labor alone and there is no minimum wage in the production of services we have $\alpha_i = \omega = 0$, $\bar{\eta}_i = \eta_i$ and $\varepsilon_i^* = \varepsilon_i \mu_i$ so

$$k = \frac{\sum \tilde{\tau}_i^{**} \eta_i p_i^c C_i + (\tilde{z}_{bi}^* - \tilde{z}_{b0}^*) \dfrac{V_i \varepsilon_i \mu_i \theta_i^v}{1+b_i}}{\sum \eta_i p_i^c C_i + \dfrac{V_i \varepsilon_i \mu_i \theta_i^v}{1+b_i}} \tag{35}$$

and the shadow price of the ith good simply becomes its reference price, $\tilde{p}_i$.

Appendix A*

SOME COMMENTS ON CHAPTER 4 OF ANANDARUP RAY'S

ISSUES IN COST BENEFIT ANALYSIS ENTITLED

"VALUATION OF TRADED AND NONTRADED GOODS"

Anandarup Ray (1984) sets out rules for shadow pricing in project evaluation. This appendix comments on selected paragraphs to help the reader master them. When presenting rules for project evaluation it is important to explain the logical bases for them, the conditions under which they apply precisely, and the circumstances under which they are likely to produce adequate approximations to the ideal rule. The need to explain the logical basis for shadow prices has become increasingly apparent from recent contributions (e.g. Blitzer, Dasgupta and Stiglitz (1981) and Bell and Devarajan (1983)) which have stressed that shadow prices depend on the adjustment mechanisms that one postulates.

First Complete Paragraph on p. 51

As we know from the appendix to Squire and van der Tak (1975) it is generally inappropriate to price traded goods with variable world prices at marginal import cost or marginal revenue. This is a legitimate practice, however, if a change in the world price of the good has no impact on goods flows within the domestic economy except for a change in the rate of growth of the

---

*Tower is the sole author of this appendix.

government's foreign exchange reserves. This would be the case if private sector participation in the market in question were subject to quantitative controls with the quota rights auctioned off. Then clearly the opportunity cost of official acquisition of one more unit of the good would simply be marginal import cost or export revenue.

Paragraph Which Straddles pp. 51 and 52

It is important to understand why it is legitimate to shadow price a non-traded good in perfectly elastic supply as the value at world prices of its traded direct and indirect inputs plus the value at shadow prices of its domestic primary factors. As Diamond-Mirrlees (1976) have noted, if a good is produced with constant returns to scale technology, there is no difference between withdrawing from the economy a unit of the good or the primary and intermediate inputs which are used in producing one unit of the good. Thus the shadow price of the former must equal the value at shadow prices of the latter, and in this way non-traded goods can be shadow priced as the value at world prices of traded goods used directly and indirectly in their production plus the shadow prices of primary factors of production used directly and indirectly in their production. Moreover this is true regardless of whether the good in question is in perfectly elastic supply.

If one wished to deal with the issue of shadow pricing primary factors here, it could be noted that under the maintained assumption of fixed product prices, so long as there are no more factors than goods, factor prices will be fixed as well. This means that the private sector will make the same income and face the same prices as before even after a change in factor supplies, so that private sector expenditure on each traded and non-traded good will be

unchanged as will private sector real income. Thus if there are more
tradeable goods than primary factors of production when a primary factor is
withdrawn from private sector production to produce an input for a project,
there will be an alteration in the production of various tradeable goods, but
no change in the production of non-tradeables. Since domestic expenditure on
each good is fixed, these changed production levels will be matched perfectly
by changed imports or exports, and the changes in official foreign exchange
reserves and hence the shadow price of the primary factor in question will be
given by the sum of the changes in this production evaluated at world
prices. Thus if we know that all of a particular factor is withdrawn from
production of a particular tradeable and that it is the only primary factor
employed there, it is an easy matter to calculate its shadow price, but in
general making such calculations is more complex since generally more than one
primary factor combine to produce each tradeable. For further discussion of
how to perform such calculations see Srinivasan and Bhagwati (1978) and Tower
(1984, chapter VI).

First Complete Paragraph on p. 52

In this paragraph it is noted that a good which is in inelastic supply
can be shadow priced as follows: its shadow price should be equal to the
value at shadow prices of the goods onto which expenditure is diverted when
the government withdraws one unit of the good from the private sector.

The reader should understand why this is a legitimate method. What sort
of tax policy is accompanying the official withdrawal of the good in question
from the economy? Are we working with Marshallian, compensated or general
equilibrium demand curves?

I interpret the implicit logic of this paragraph as follows. Pretend that the government levies lump sum taxes or subsidies so as to leave each individual as well off as before it purchased the non-traded good in question. This means that we will be concerned solely with movements along the compensated demand curve. It also means that the sole cost to the economy will be the foreign exchange cost which (assuming fixed world prices) will be equal to the increase in net imports evaluated at foreign currency prices. If demand for all non-traded goods and traded goods with variable world prices is unchanged, the output of all goods will be fixed and the foreign exchange cost can be calculated as the value of increased expenditure on the various traded goods multiplied by the conversion factor for each traded good. Thus we have expressed the cost of acquiring a unit of the non-traded good as a foreign exchange loss, and consequently this foreign exchange loss is its shadow price.

First Paragraph on p. 53

This paragraph implicitly assumes that there is only one non-traded good or that the demands for and supplies of all other non-traded goods are independent of government acquisition of the non-traded good in question. Also N implicitly refers to the compensated demand elasticity. One way to understand this paragraph is to recognize that the shadow price of the non-traded good is equal to the extra foreign exchange used to keep the private sector at the same level of welfare as before, and then to note that in the special case where our non-traded good substitutes in consumption for a batch of traded goods only and in production for some other batch of traded goods, the formula provided indicates the extra amount of foreign exchange used. This formula is usable only under the very restrictive assumptions mentioned above, and consequently its limited usefulness should be emphasized along with the conceptual nature of how we are shadow pricing everything as its opportunity cost in foreign exchange, because this latter is important for understanding the meaning of a conversion factor.

Second Paragraph on p. 53

The shadow price of an exportable is not marginal export revenue except when the world price is fixed or domestic excess supply is perfectly inelastic.

Chapter 4's Appendix B

It should be emphasized that all of these formulae assume that all goods are traded at fixed world prices except for the one good in question. Moreover the E in $(1+E)^{-1}$ in equation (4.2a) should be t.

The implicit model in this annex is the following. There is a representative resident of the country and the government adjusts taxes and subsidies to maintain him at a given level of welfare. Then each item is shadow priced as the amount of foreign exchange required to maintain welfare at the same level after withdrawal of one unit of the item in question from the private sector. Since welfare never changes, the demand elasticity in question must be a compensated one, in both the derivation of shadow prices of goods which are traded at variable world prices and also non-traded goods.

Appendix B*

NOTES ON SQUIRE AND VAN DER TAK'S (1975, pp. 144-145) FORMULAE FOR SHADOW

PRICING EXPORTABLES WITH VARIABLE WORLD PRICES AND NON TRADEABLES

The formulae on page 144 and 145 of Squire and van der Tak are deceptive-
ly simple, because interpreting some of the terms in them is tricky. The η_d
in these expressions is neither a Marshallian nor a compensated demand
elasticity. It is the percentage change in quantity demanded per percentage
change in price given that real and nominal incomes of producers and real
incomes of consumers are altering in response to the price changes in
question. Thus it is a general euilibrium elasticity. Similarly, the
β_1 and β_2 reflect the changes in purchases of the traded commodities due to
compensated price changes and the changes in real incomes generated by these
price changes. These β's then are different from Ray's (1984, ch.4) β
which reflects the changes in the purchases of tradeables due to a compensated
price change. To derive η_d, β_1 and β_2 from the underlying compensated
demand elasticities, marginal propensities to spend, and tariffs is a problem
which is not conceptually difficult, but has been brushed over in these
derivations. To highlight the differences in the two approaches we now derive
β_1 from the others.

Pretend that all goods except for the nontraded good in question are
traded at fixed world prices with t_i being the advalorem import tariff or
export subsidy attached to the ith traded good and p_i being the domestic
price. Let C^N be initial consumption of the nontradeable. An increase in the

---

*Tower is the sole author of this appendix.

price of the non-tradeable of dp^N causes consumers' real income to rise by $dy = -C^N dp^N$ (assuming no consumers are also producers) and if consumers had been compensated, their expenditure on other goods would have risen by $\sum p_i dC_i = -p^N dC_N = \eta^c C^N dp^N$, where η^c is the compensated elasticity of demand for the non-tradeable and the $\sum$ throughout our analysis runs over the traded goods only.

Define β^y as $\sum m_i/(1+t_i)$ where m_i is the marginal propensity to spend out of income on the ith traded good and t_i is the ad valorem import tariff or export subsidy on it. Note incidentally that if all $t_i = 0$, $\beta^y = 1 - m^N$ where m^N is the marginal propensity to spend on the non-traded good. Also define β^c as

$$\frac{\sum p_i(dC_i/dp^N)/(1+t_i)}{\sum_i p_i(dC_i/dp^N)} \tag{1}$$

where dC_i/dp^N is the change in consumption of the ith good per unit change in the price of the non-traded good along a compensated demand curve. This means that the change in foreign exchange used up can be written as

$$[-\beta^y + \eta^c \beta^c]C^N dp^N. \tag{2}$$

Squire and van der Tak's notation for the same term is

$$\beta_1(\eta_d - 1)C^N dp^N. \tag{3}$$

where since we are analyzing consumers of the good who don't produce any of it themselves, the η_d is a Marshallian elasticity. Thus $(\eta_d-1)C^N dp^N$ is the extra amount of money that consumers have to spend on traded goods. The Slutsky decomposition enables us to write η_d as $\eta_d = \eta^c + m^N$. Thus we can solve for Squire and van der Tak's β_1 as

$$\beta_1 = \frac{-\beta^y + \eta^c \beta^c}{\eta^c + m^N - 1}, \qquad (4)$$

where β^c is the consumption conversion factor used in Ray (1984). Note that when the m's in β^y are proportional to the $p_i dC_i/dp^N$ in β^c, β_1 and β^c will be identical. However, in general they will be different. Finally note from section II that β^y is not the reciprocal of the shadow price of foreign exchange except in the special case where the marginal propensity to consume the non traded good is zero.

Appendix C*

ON TERRY A. POWERS' (ed.) <u>ESTIMATING ACCOUNTING</u>
<u>PRICES FOR PROJECT APPRAISAL</u>

This volume (Powers 1981) consists of three chapters which outline the techniques used to calculate accounting prices followed by four case studies which apply these methods to various countries. The problem is that the volume is very difficult to understand because the conceptual general equilibrium model underlying the fundamental logic behind the calculations is not explained. We are given rules for calculating accounting price ratios, but the assumptions about the economy for which these rules are appropriate are not explained. Consequently it is difficult to determine whether the logical basis for these calculations is sound. The difficulty is that there is virtually always some assumption that will justify any calculation.

For example, one finds oneself asking questions raised in Srinivasan and Bhagwati (1978), Bertrand (1979), and Bhagwati and Wan (1979), but these are not addressed in the volume.

Much of the logic behind the derivation of accounting prices relies on Diamond and Mirrlees (1976) but this piece is not cited. For example, the fact that the shadow price of a unit of output is equal to the sum of the values at shadow prices of the inputs necessary to produce it holds only when the production process is first degree homogeneous, and in that circumstance there is a compelling rationale for this result. However we are not told about the restriction on the Diamond-Mirrlees result.

_____

*Tower is the sole author of this appendix.

In much of the analysis it appears that Powers assumes that labor is the only primary input, because he does not recognize that if there is more than one primary factor, when labor is removed from a sector, excess supplies of other primary factors will be created which will need to be absorbed elsewhere, as in Srinivasan and Bhagwati (1978). However, it is difficult to tell whether he is making that assumption or being inconsistent.

Accounting prices, like any product of second best welfare analysis are very sensitive to the particular adjustment mechanisms assumed. It is essential to indicate the relationships which are being assumed in the presentation of shadow price calculations.

What we need is simple logically consistent general equilibrium models for calculating shadow prices, rather than ad hoc rules. From the very simplest models simple rules do emerge, but these have a clear cut logical foundation.[1]

---

[1]There is much to be said for employing a model like that of Jenkins and Kuo (1983) which is a very straight forward general equilibrium model with fixed stocks of resources, labor and capital and allows for differences between goods produced by domestic and foreign firms.

Appendix D

SHADOW PRICING IN AN ECONOMY WITH A UNIVERSAL

MINIMUM WAGE AND UNEMPLOYMENT

In the text's development of shadow price expressions we have avoided the use of matrix methods. This seems sensible in order to foster an intuitive understanding of the issues involved and to provide frameworks for back of the envelope calculations. However this does impose limits on the degree of complexity of the models that one can build. In this appendix and the next we use matrix methods to derive shadow prices as an indication of the sorts of calculation that can potentially be performed. In this appendix we consider an economy with a universal minimum wage and unemployment while in the next we postulate full employment.

The commodity balance condition is

$$dC = dQ - \begin{bmatrix} dE \\ \cdot \\ 0 \\ \cdot \end{bmatrix} + \bar{Q} \tag{1}$$

where $\begin{bmatrix} dE \\ \cdot \\ 0 \\ \cdot \end{bmatrix}$ is a column vector, the top T elements of which refer to the changes in net exports of the T traded goods, and the bottom H elements of which are zeros and refer to the H non-traded or home goods. Also, $\bar{Q}$ is a (1 x N) column vector of autonomous increases in endowments of the N goods consumed.

We assume fixed world prices so that the balance of payments equilibrium is defined by

$$p*'dE + \bar{F} = 0 \tag{2}$$

where p* is a column vector of world prices and a prime denotes a transpose.

Each good is produced with a first degree homogeneous production function that combines intermediate inputs and a value-added aggregate in fixed proportions, where the value-added aggregate is a first degree homogeneous function of labor, which is mobile between industries, and a fixed factor, taken to be land or capital. Moreover labor and the fixed factor are substitutable for one another in producing the value-added aggregate.

Net output, Q, is related to gross output X, by

$$dQ = [I - A]dX \qquad\qquad (3)$$

where Q and X are the (N x 1) column vectors of net and gross outputs and A is the domestic physical input/output matrix.

A minimum wage is assumed to prevail in all industries, and some labor is unemployed. Thus, with a frozen wage rate equation 7 from chapter II of Tower (1984) becomes

$$[I - \theta']\hat{p} - [\tfrac{1}{\varepsilon X}]^D dX = 0 \qquad\qquad (4)$$

where $\hat{p}$ is the (N x 1) column vector of proportional changes in domestic prices and we have ignored excise taxes here, so p_i is the price of i to both domestic producers and consumers, θ' is the transpose of θ which is the matrix made up of θ_{ij} which is the share of good i in the production of j in the initial equilibrium, and $[\tfrac{1}{\varepsilon X}]^D$ is the diagonal matrix of $\tfrac{1}{\varepsilon_i X_i}$ where ε is the elasticity of the supply of output with respect to its own price.

We write the demand functions as

$$dC = \beta\hat{p} + (m/p)dy \tag{5}$$

where β is the N x N matrix of pure substitution terms, with the ijth being $\eta_{ij}C_i$ where η_{ij} is the compensated elasticity of demand for the ith good with respect to the jth price, m/p is the N x 1 column vector of marginal propensities to consume out of real income and dy is the change in real income, defined so that at initial prices real and nominal incomes are identical.

Since world prices and trade taxes and subsidies are fixed the domestic prices of the T tradeables are fixed. Thus we can write

$$\hat{p} = \left[\cdot \overset{0}{\underset{h}{\vdots}} \cdot \right] \tag{6}$$

where 0 is a (T x 1) column vector of 0's and $\hat{h}$ is the (H x 1) column vector of proportional changes in non-traded (home) goods prices.

In order to shadow price the economy's goods with the foreign exchange numeraire we constrain dy to equal zero and solve for $-\bar{F}$ as a linear function of $\bar{Q}$. The coefficient of $\bar{Q}_i$ then gives the savings in foreign exchange which making available one more unit of $\bar{Q}_i$ would permit, if real income is to be left unchanged, which we can interpret as the shadow price of Q_i. This is the technique we now proceed to use.

Combining (3) and (4) yields

$$dQ = \Psi\hat{p} \tag{7}$$

where $\Psi = [I - A][\varepsilon X]^D[I - \theta']$.

Combining (1), (5), (6) and (7) with

$$dy = 0 \qquad\qquad (7')$$

yields

$$\Phi \begin{bmatrix} 0 \\ \cdot \hat{h} \cdot \end{bmatrix} = -\begin{bmatrix} dE \\ \cdot 0 \cdot \end{bmatrix} + \bar{Q} \qquad\qquad (8)$$

where $\Phi = \beta - \Psi = \begin{bmatrix} \Phi_{TT} & \vdots & \Phi_{TH} \\ \cdots & \cdots & \cdots \\ \Phi_{HT} & \vdots & \Phi_{HH} \end{bmatrix}$

with Φ_{TH} having dimensions T x H

and Φ_{HH} having dimensions H x H.

Equation (8) can be rewitten as

$$\Phi_{TH} \hat{h} = -dE + \bar{Q}_T \qquad\qquad (9)$$

and

$$\Phi_{HH} \hat{h} = \bar{Q}_H \qquad\qquad (10)$$

where $\bar{Q}_T$ and $\bar{Q}_H$ are the autonomous increases in endowments of the various tradeable and non-tradeable goods respectively, so that

$$\bar{Q} = \begin{bmatrix} \bar{Q}_T \\ \cdot \cdot \cdot \\ \bar{Q}_H \end{bmatrix}. \qquad\qquad (11)$$

Solving (10) for $\hat{h}$ and substituting into (9) yields

$$dE = -\Phi_{TH} \Phi_{HH}^{-1} \bar{Q}_H + \bar{Q}_T \qquad\qquad (12)$$

which is substituted into (2) to yield

$$\bar{F} = p^{*\prime} \{ [\Phi_{TH} \Phi_{HH}^{-1} \bar{Q}_H] - \bar{Q}_T \}. \qquad\qquad (13)$$

There are several points of interest which emerge from (13). One is that the shadow price of the ith tradeable is simply its world price. A second is that to calculate the shadow prices of the various non-tradeables, i.e. each conversion factor, we need to know all of the elements of Ψ as well as the last H columns of β. In other words, we need to know all physical input/output coefficients, the shares of all intermediate inputs and value-addeds in the production of each good and all initial gross outputs. Also, we need to know all initial consumption levels as well as the compensated partial elasticity of demand for each good with respect to the price of each non-traded good. Finally, shadow pricing labor was no problem in this model since perpetual unemployment constrained it to be equal to zero.

Appendix E

SHADOW PRICING IN A FULLY EMPLOYED ECONOMY

As a final exercise, we find the shadow prices of goods, foreign exchange and labor when a flexible wage rate enables labor to be employed continually. Our model consists of the equations used in the previous section except that equation 7 from chapter II of Tower (1984) leads us to replace (D4) with

$$[I - \theta']\hat{p} - \theta^v\hat{w} - \left[\frac{1}{\epsilon X}\right]^D dX = 0 \tag{1}$$

where θ^v is a (N x 1) column vector of the shares of value added in output and $\hat{w}$ is the proportional change in the economy-wide wage rate. Also from equation 6 of chapter II of Tower (1984)

$$dQ = \lambda^D dL \tag{2}$$

where λ^D is an (N x N) diagonal matrix with the i, ith element equal to

$$\frac{X_i v_{Li}}{L_i}$$

where

   v_{Li} is the share of labor in value added in industry i

   L_i is labor in industry i and

   dL is the (N x 1) column vector of changes in labor allocated to the
          various industries.

Finally, full employment dictates

$$UdL = \bar{L} \tag{3}$$

where $\bar{L}$ is the autonomous increase in the supply of labor services and U is a 1 x N row vector of 1's.

Combining (D3) and (1) yields

$$dQ = \Psi\hat{p} + \Omega\hat{w} \tag{4}$$

where Ψ is defined in (D7), $\Omega = -[I - A]\varepsilon X\theta^V$ and $eX\theta^V$ is an N x 1 column vector. Combining (D), (D5), (D6), (D7') and (4) yields

$$\Phi\left[\begin{matrix}0\\ \cdot\hat{\wedge}\cdot\\ h\end{matrix}\right] = -\left[\begin{matrix}dE\\ \cdot\hat{\circ}\cdot\\ 0\end{matrix}\right] + \bar{Q} + \Omega\hat{w} \tag{5}$$

where Φ is defined in (D8). Combining (2) with (4) and (D6) yields

$$\Psi\left[\begin{matrix}0\\ \cdot\hat{\wedge}\cdot\\ h\end{matrix}\right] + \Omega\hat{w} = \lambda^D dL. \tag{6}$$

Equations (3) and (6) combine to yield

$$U(\lambda^{-1})^D\left[\Psi\left[\begin{matrix}0\\ \cdot\hat{\wedge}\cdot\\ h\end{matrix}\right] + \Omega\hat{w}\right] = \bar{L}. \tag{7}$$

Equation (5) can be rewritten as

$$\Phi_{TH}\hat{h} = -dE + \bar{Q}_T + \Omega_T\hat{w} \tag{8}$$

plus

$$\Phi_{HH}\hat{h} = \bar{Q}_H + \Omega_H\hat{w} \tag{9}$$

where $\Omega = \left[\begin{matrix}\Omega_T\\ \cdot\cdot\cdot\\ \Omega_H\end{matrix}\right].$

Solving (9) and substituting it into (7) yields

$$\hat{w} = \alpha\{\bar{L} + b_1\bar{Q}_H\}$$ (10)

where $\alpha = \left[U(\lambda^{-1})^D \Psi_H \Phi_{HH}^{-1}\Omega_H + \Omega\right]^{-1}$

$b_1 = -U(\lambda^{-1})^D \Psi_H \Phi_{HH}^{-1}$ and

Ψ_H is the matrix of the H right-hand columns of Ψ.
Substituting this back into (9) yields

$$\hat{h} = b_2\bar{Q}_H + b_3\bar{L}$$ (11)

where $b_2 = \Phi_{HH}^{-1}(1 + \Omega_H\alpha b_1)$ and

$b_3 = \Phi_{HH}^{-1}\Omega_H\alpha.$

Then substituting (10) and (11) into (8) to solve for dE, and substituting the result into (D2) yields

$$\bar{F} = p^{*\prime}\left[b_4\bar{Q}_H + b_5\bar{L} - \bar{Q}_T\right]$$ (12)

where $b_4 = \Phi_{TH}b_2 - \Omega_T\alpha b_1$ and

$b_5 = \Phi_{TH}b_3 - \Omega_T\alpha.$

The only readily apparent conclusion that emerges from (12) is the useful check that again, the shadow price of the ith tradeable with the price of foreign exchange as the numeraire is simply its world price. While the derivation in this case was somewhat more complex than in the previous one, it was still manageable and presented no conceptual difficulties.

REFERENCES

Bacha, E. and Taylor L., "Foreign Exchange Shadow Prices: A Critical Review of Current Literature," Quarterly Journal of Economics 85 (May 1971): 197-224.

Balassa, B., "Estimating the Shadow Price of Foreign Exchange in Project Appraisal," Oxford Economic Papers 26 (July 1974): 147-68.

Bell, C. and Devarajan, S., "Shadow Prices for Project Evaluation Under Alternative Macroeconomic Specifications," Quarterly Journal of Economics 97 (August 1983): 457-477.

Bertrand, T. J., "Welfare Indexes With Interindustry Flows: Comment," Journal of Political Economy 80 (December 1972): 796-800.

Bertrand, T. J. "The Shadow Exchange Rate in an Economy with Trade Restrictions," Oxford Economic Papers 26 (July 1974): 69-79.

Bertrand, T. J., "Shadow Pricing in Distorted Economies," American Economic Review 69 (December 1979): 902-914.

Bhagwati, J. N., Brecher, R. A., and Hatta, T., "The Paradoxes of Immiserizing Growth and Donor-Enriching (Recipient-Immiserizing) Transfers: A Tale of Two Literatures," Weltwirtschaftliches Archiv 120 (1984): 228-243.

Bhagwati, J., Ramaswami, V. K., and Srinivasan, T. N., "Domestic Distortions, Tariffs, and the Theory of Optimum Subsidy: Some Further Results," Journal of Political Economy 77 (November/December 1969): 1005-10.

Bhagwati, J. N. and Srinivasan, T. N., "The Evaluation of Projects at World Prices Under Trade Distortions: Quantitative Restrictions, Monopoly Power in Trade and Nontraded Goods," International Economic Review 22 (June 1981): 385-399.

Bhagwati, J. N. and Wan, H., "The 'Stationarity' of Shadow Prices of Factors in Project Evaluation With and Without Distortions," American Economic Review 69 (June 1979): 261-273.

Blitzer, C. R., Dasgupta, P. and Stiglitz, J., "Project Evaluation and the Foreign Exchange Constraint," Economic Journal (1981).

Diamond, P. A. and Mirrlees, J. A., "Private Constant Returns and Public Shadow Prices," Review of Economic Studies 43 (February 1976): 41-48.

Harberger, A. C., "Basic Needs Versus Distributional Weights in Social Cost Benefit Analysis," mimeo, 1978a.

Harberger, A. C., "On the Use of Distributional Weights in Social Cost Benefit Analysis," Journal of Political Economy, Supplement, April 1978b.

Jenkins, G. P. and Kuo, C-Y., "On Measuring the Social Opportunity Cost of Foreign Exchange," Canadian Journal of Economics forthcoming.

Little, I. M. D. and Mirrlees, J. A., Project Appraisal and Planning for Developing Countries, Basic Books, Inc., 1974.

Mashayeki, A., Shadow Prices for Project Appraisal in Turkey, World Bank Staff Working Paper, No. 392, May 1980.

Postlewaite, A., and Webb, M., "The Effect of International Commodity Transfers: The Possibility of Transferor-Benefiting, Transferee-Harming Transfers," Journal of Interantional Economics 16 (May, 1984).

Powers, T. A. (ed.), Estimating Accounting Prices for Project Appraisal, Inter-American Development Bank, 1981.

Pursell, G., "Estimating Shadow Exchange Rates: The Ivory Coast," World Bank, Mimeo, 1978.

Ray, A., Issues in Cost Benefit Analysis, Johns Hopkins University Press, 1984.

Scott, M. F. G., "How to Use and Estimate Shadow Exchange Rates," Oxford Economic Papers, 26 (July 1974): 169-84.

Sieper, E., "The Structure of General Equilibrium Shadow Pricing Rules for a Tax-Distorted Economy," Department of Economics, Australian National University and Center of Policy Studies, Monash university, Mimeo, October 1980; revised January 1981.

Smith, A., "Some Simple Results on the Gains from Trade, from Growth and from Public Production," Journal of International Economics 13 (November 1982): 215-230.

Squire, L. and van der Tak, H. G., Economic Analysis of Projects, Johns Hopkins University Press, 1975.

Srinivasan, T. N., "General Equilibrium Theory, Project Evaluation and Economic Development," Ch. 14 of M. Gersovitz, et al. (eds.), The Theory and Experience of Economic Development: Essays in Honor of Sir W. Arthur Lewis George Allen and Unwin, Ltd., 1982.

Srinivasan, T. N. and Bhagwati, J. N., "Shadow Prices of Project Selection in the Presence of Distortions: Effective Rates of Protection and Domestic Resource Costs," Journal of Political Economy 86 (February 1978): 97-114; chapter 17 of J. N. Bhagwati (1981).

Tower, E., "The Geometry of Community Indifference Curves," Weltwirtschaftlishes Archiv, Heft 4, 1979, 680-700.

Tower, E. Effective Protection, Domestic Resource Cost and Shadow Prices: A General Equilibrium Perspective, World Bank Staff Working Paper, No. 664, September 1984.

Yano, M., "Welfare Aspects of the Transfer Problem," Journal of International Economics 15 (November 1983).